BORN TO BE *Blessed*

RELEASING GOD'S PROMISES INTO THE LIVES OF THOSE YOU LOVE

JOHN HAGEE

WORTHY
PUBLISHING

The publisher wishes to acknowledge that a portion of this material is adapted from *The Power of the Prophetic Blessing* by John Hagee.

Published by Worthy Publishing, a division of Worthy Media, Inc., 134 Franklin Road, Suite 200, Brentwood, Tennessee 37027.

HELPING PEOPLE EXPERIENCE THE HEART OF GOD

eBook available at worthypublishing.com

Library of Congress Control Number: 2013931706

Portions of this material were first published in *The Power of the Prophetic Blessing* © 2012 by John Hagee. Published by Worthy Publishing, Brentwood, Tennessee.

For foreign and subsidiary rights, contact Riggins International Rights Services, Inc.; rigginsrights.com

Published in association with Ted Squires Agency, Nashville, Tennessee

ISBN: 978-1-61795-190-9 (hardcover w/jacket)
ISBN: 978-1-61795-232-6 (international edition)

Cover Design: Christopher Tobias, Tobias' Outerwear for Books
Meadow Photo: © MOF/Getty Images
Sea Photo: © Warren Goldswain/Fotolia
Interior Design and Typesetting: Kimberly Sagmiller, Fudge Creative

Printed in the United States of America
13 14 15 16 17 18 QGFF 8 7 6 5 4 3 2 1

TABLE OF CONTENTS

You Were Born to Be Blessed!

I have a message of hope and truth for everyone reading this book who wants to live a fulfilled and successful life: God Almighty has declared that every one of His children is *born to be blessed!*

The Prophetic Blessing is a spoken declaration by a spiritual authority over the life of an individual. The words of the blessing carry the power to control and direct the life of the person over whom they have been spoken. The Prophetic Blessing will revolutionize your life and the lives of your family members—children, nieces, nephews, grandchildren, godchildren—no matter their age or current circumstances, enabling them to rise to a higher level of accomplishment and creating spiritual, physical, emotional, and relational prosperity.

The power and permanence of the Prophetic Blessing have been clearly charted over the centuries in sacred Scripture. The Jewish people have obeyed the principles and received the benefits of the blessing;

however, its potential has been sadly overlooked by most Christians for over two thousand years. This transforming supernatural blessing spoken by spiritual authority has the power to sculpt your life and the lives of your children for today, tomorrow, and forever!

When I taught the power of the Prophetic Blessing to my congregation, I directed every father and mother to lay hands on his or her children and speak a blessing over them. I instructed them to personally profess the future accomplishments they desired for each child.

Lives were immediately changed. Weeping could be heard from every corner of the sanctuary. Testimonies began pouring in of sons and daughters whose lives were transformed by the power of the Prophetic Blessing spoken over them by their spiritual authority. School grades improved; behavioral problems and low self-esteem vanished! Their children walked and talked with an air of confidence they had never demonstrated before.

The power of the Prophetic Blessing has changed the course of our ministry and positively impacted our congregation, our nation, and the nations of the world with supernatural results that were beyond our most aspiring dreams or imagination. And it can transform your family too!

I've written *Born to Be Blessed* to teach you how to release the power of the Prophetic Blessing into your family. Your children were born to be blessed—and you, as their parent or spiritual authority, can proclaim that blessing in accordance with the sacred Scriptures and watch it become reality in the lives of those whom you love.

In part 1 of this book, I'll explain the Prophetic Blessing, show you how God's blessing dramatically changed lives throughout Scripture, and then teach you how to release the God-ordained Prophetic Blessing in your own family through the Spoken Word and physical touch. Along the way, I'll share powerful, encouraging stories of families—just like yours—who have experienced the profoundly transforming power of the Prophetic Blessing. In part 2, I'll share several specific proclamations you can speak over your children and loved ones in order to release the supernatural power of the Prophetic Blessing in your home and family.

You don't need to wait any longer; you have the power to turn your family around today! Regardless of your family's situation or how hopeless you may feel at this very moment, declare that you will no longer accept a mediocre existence for your family. Begin thinking of your children as successful in everything they put their hand to. I encourage you to end all destructive speech about your children, their current circumstances, and their future. Instead, look at a family picture and say out loud, "My children were born to be blessed!"

You don't need to search any further for the answers to the challenges of your life; you just need to read this book, believing that you and your children have the potential to lead a blessed life . . . because you were *born to be blessed!*

PART 1

꒦꒷

THE PROPHETIC BLESSING

CHAPTER 1

WHAT IS THE PROPHETIC *Blessing?*

W hen we encounter a stranger who sneezes in the elevator, most of us instinctively say, "God bless you!" A Hispanic farewell proclaims a blessing for a safe journey through the phrase "*Vaya con Dios*." Even Boaz of the Old Testament greeted his reapers with a blessing: "The LORD be with you" (Ruth 2:4). There are many ways man desires to extend God's blessing upon others.

These kinds of statements may seek God's favor upon something or someone; however, they are not examples of the God-ordained Priestly Blessing, nor are they an impartation of the Prophetic Blessing. Let us begin by defining the difference between the Priestly Blessing and the Prophetic Blessing.

THE PRIESTLY BLESSING

The book of Numbers houses within its pages what is often referred to as the Lord's Prayer of the Old Testament. The Lord commanded Moses to instruct Aaron and his sons to bless the children of Israel by placing His Name upon them. Aaron and his sons comprised the priesthood of Israel, and therefore this passage is referred to as the Priestly Blessing.

This profound proclamation is one of God's gifts to His own, for within its sacred text He defines the essence of the word *blessing*. In its promises, we can see the heart of God and experience a small portion of the great love He has for us.

Read aloud the transforming promises from God to you in the Priestly Blessing:

And the Lord *spoke to Moses, saying: "Speak to Aaron and his sons, saying, 'This is the way you shall bless the children of Israel. Say to them:*

"The Lord *bless you and keep you;*
The Lord *make His face shine upon you,*

And be gracious to you;
The LORD lift up His countenance upon you,
And give you peace.'"

"So they shall put My name on the children of Israel,
and I will bless them." (Numbers 6:22–27)

The Priestly Blessing was not just for Moses, Aaron, and the elite members of the tribe of Levi; it was intended for *every person on the face of the earth.* That means the Priestly Blessing is for you—and for your children.

This awesome promise can only come from an awesome God. This blessing comes to you directly from the Creator of heaven and earth. The prophet Isaiah called Him "Wonderful, Counselor, Mighty God, Everlasting Father, Prince of Peace" (Isaiah 9:6). Sacred Scripture calls Him the great "I AM" and the Good Shepherd of the sheep (Exodus 3:14; John 10:11). The mighty source of blessing that knows no limit is Emmanuel, "God with us," and the hope of glory. He is the immortal and invisible God. He can restore your dead marriage, heal your diseased body, and renew your distressed mind. He has promised to make you the head and not the tail. He will give you houses you didn't build, vineyards you didn't plant, and wells you didn't dig. He will plant you by rivers of living water, and whatsoever you do will prosper! He is the Lord who gives you the power to get wealth.

The verb *to bless* in Hebrew is related to the noun *knee* and can mean "to adore on bended knee" (Psalm 95:6) or "to present something of value to another." Nearly every Hebrew blessing begins with this word, for God deserves all of man's praise and adoration (Psalm 113:2). Through the Priestly Blessing, God is bestowing His favor on His creation—mortal man. How humbling! This is the purest expression of His mercy and grace.[1] God blesses His children by giving us life and provision; we bless Him through our praise and by living our lives to the fullest.

THE PROPHETIC BLESSING

Let us now briefly distinguish between the Priestly Blessing and the Prophetic Blessing. While the Priestly Blessing is the direct proclamation from *God* over man as stated in Numbers 6, the Prophetic Blessing is the spoken declaration from God's *spiritual authority* concerning the life of an individual. Once the Priestly Blessing has been spoken over the recipient, then the Prophetic Blessing follows. Unlike the Priestly Blessing, the Prophetic Blessing is unique to every person imparting it as well as to the one receiving it.

> *And [Jacob] blessed [his twelve sons]; he blessed each one according to his own blessing. (Genesis 49:28)*

The scriptural use of the word *blessing* has several connotations in the Hebrew language. When God blesses man, it is to bestow good health, abundant success, and prosperity, both materially and spiritually. When man blesses God, it is presented in the forms of thanksgiving, reverence, obedience, praise, and worship. When a man blesses his fellow believer, he recites the Priestly Blessing of Numbers 6:22–27 and then proclaims the Holy Spirit-inspired Prophetic Blessing. As you read *Born to Be Blessed,* you will discover how this divine proclamation, guided by the Holy Spirit, will supernaturally form your life and the lives of those you love.

THE POWER TO SCULPT
YOUR FUTURE

The Prophetic Blessing spoken by God's delegated authority has had a profound impact on my life and ministry. We held a week of services in 1987 when we dedicated Cornerstone Church. My father, Reverend William Bythel Hagee, spoke into existence the following Prophetic Blessing over me through his dedication prayer:

Our Father, which art in heaven, we come before You today with our hearts overflowing with gratitude for Your faithfulness. "Except the Lord build the house, they labor in vain that build it." This house of worship is Your doing, and it is precious in our sight.

Heavenly Father, accept the work of our hands as a sacrifice of praise to Your holy Name. Let this house of prayer be a lighthouse to a world groping in spiritual darkness. Let Your Word go forth from this place to the uttermost parts of the earth and let sons and daughters be born into the kingdom of God without number.

May it be to us and to our children through all the

coming years a shrine of blessed memories. May it be a refuge from the cares and burdens of life. May it be a shelter in the times of the storm. Fill this sanctuary with Your Holy Spirit and fill us with Your love, peace, and joy. As the erection of the temple is in vain without the consecration of the people, we offer our lives to You today anew as Your servants, Lord. Let Your Word abide in our hearts. May we here be changed into Your own glorious image. Let us remember that You are the Cornerstone of this church. You are the precious One. You are the Rock of our salvation.

Our Father, bless those who minister here. May they be vessels fitted for the Master's use. Give them strength for the journey. Anoint their ministry to guide the souls of men in paths of righteousness. When tired, sin-sick, hungry hearts walk through these doors, let them find Living Water and the Bread of Life. Hear our prayer, O Lord, our God, our King, and our Redeemer. These things we ask in the precious Name of our Lord and Savior, Jesus Christ. Amen. [2]

I am deeply moved every time I read this powerful proclamation over my life. Why? Because it was spoken in faith by God's delegated authority over my life; it was spoken according to God's Word; and I received it and have done what is necessary to see its contents come to pass.

My wife, Diana, and I attended the International Christian Businessmen's Conference at Oral Roberts University in 1991, held in the Mabee Center. I was serving on the Board of Regents at Oral Roberts University at the time and was also one of the speakers at the conference. Little did we know that the final session would be a moment in time that would help sculpt our future.

As Diana and I sat in the front row, the speaker taught from Habakkuk 2:2–3, which states:

> *Write the vision*
> *And make it plain on tablets,*
> *That he may run who reads it.*
> *For the vision is yet for an appointed time;*
> *But at the end it will speak, and it will not lie.*
> *Though it tarries, wait for it;*
> *Because it will surely come,*
> *It will not tarry.*

We listened to the speaker develop the concept of writing down all the things we would like to accomplish in the future. I reached for my Bible, and Diana and I agreed to write down the vision we had for our lives and make a profession of faith that God would bring it to pass. We did not know at the time that everything we wrote in that Bible that day would come to pass over the next twenty years exactly as it was written.

Our proclamation for the future:

To build a national television ministry that would reach America and the world for the purpose of preaching all the gospel to all the world.

To build a New Testament church filled with the signs and wonders of the New Testament that would bless the city of San Antonio and America.

To build a Conference Center that would receive the nations of the world to restore, unite, train, and teach the lost, the brokenhearted, and the discouraged; heal the sick; and offer deliverance to the oppressed.

All of this to be done to the glory of God

the Father and His Son, Jesus Christ, through the power of the Holy Spirit.

—18 JUNE 1991, ICBM CONFERENCE, ORAL ROBERTS UNIVERSITY

I have this vision statement framed in my office. My life is living proof that the Prophetic Blessing has the power to establish your future when it is in agreement with the Word and the will of God.

Get a vision of what you want God to do with your life, your ministry, your family, your children and grand-children. Dare to believe that Jesus Christ is the High Priest of your Prophetic Blessing. Have faith that He will lend His power and authority to fulfill the bless-ing over your family in agreement with His Word. Live in accordance with your prophetic proclamation and watch God act on your behalf!

Chapter 2

THE PROPHETIC *Blessing* IN SCRIPTURE

It is God's passionate desire to bless you. His greatest glory is to bring joy, love, and peace to all who will become a part of the kingdom of God. God's blessing is a central theme of the Bible. Throughout the pages of Scripture, God blessed His children with His unmerited favor and spoke prophetic blessings over their lives.

The first thing God did for Adam and Eve in the Garden of Eden was to bless them. As we turn the pages of sacred Scripture, we see this theme continue as God blessed Abraham, Isaac, Jacob, and His prophets.

God's own Son, Jesus Christ, opened His mouth and the *ruach* (supernatural breath) came forth just as it did in the Garden of Eden when God the Father breathed life into Adam. This same *ruach* blessed God's people in the Sermon on the Mount, where Jesus mapped out the royal road for all men to be supremely blessed.

In this chapter, let's take a closer look at the power of the Prophetic Blessing in Scripture.

THE PROPHETIC BLESSING OF ADAM AND EVE

In the genesis of time, a loving and gracious God created a garden of such splendor that the mind of man cannot begin to imagine the half of its grandeur. And in this garden, God spoke a blessing over His creation. Genesis 1:28 records these words spoken to Adam and Eve:

> *Then God blessed them, and God said to them, "Be fruitful and multiply; fill the earth and subdue it; have dominion over the fish of the sea, over the birds of the air, and over every living thing that moves on the earth."*

"Be fruitful and multiply" is both a blessing and a command. The union of one man with one woman is intended to produce children. This command is the antithesis of the pro-abortion and pro-homosexual agenda. It is not possible for two men or two women to produce a child. God created male and female, making marriage between two men or two women a clear violation of the law of God. God will only bless the union He created; therefore He blessed the union of marriage between a man and a woman with children, as recorded by King David in Psalm 127:3–5:

> *Children are a heritage from the LORD,*
> *The fruit of the womb is a reward.*
> *Like arrows in the hand of a warrior,*
> *So are the children of one's youth.*
> *Happy is the man who has his quiver full of them;*
> *They shall not be ashamed,*
> *But shall speak with their enemies in the gate.*

We in America do not treat our children as rewards or respect them for the blessing God intended them to be. They are instead exploited through child pornography, abused through neglect, and killed through abortion. Because of these transgressions, a portion of our nation's future has been destroyed. Since *Roe v. Wade*, more than fifty-four million children have been murdered in the wombs of their mothers between 1973 and 2008.[1] A potential Mozart, an Einstein, a future president of the United States, schoolteachers, firefighters, police officers, loving mothers, and compassionate fathers have been eliminated from our society because we have failed to honor God's command and blessing to be fruitful and multiply.

GOD'S BLESSING OF ABRAHAM

The next blessing given in Scripture was God's blessing of Abraham, found in Genesis 12:1–3, creating the nation of Israel and what became known as the Jewish people:

> Now the LORD had said to Abram: *"Get out of your country, from your family and from your father's house, to a land [Israel] that I will show you. I will make you a great nation; I will bless you. And make your name great; and you shall be a blessing. I will bless those who bless you [Israel and the Jewish people],*

*and I will curse him who curses you; and in you all
the families of the earth shall be blessed."*

This Prophetic Blessing—assuring the creation and
establishment of the state of Israel—is the theological
cornerstone of the greatest controversy in the Middle
East, from the time of Abraham to the twenty-first century. However, the fact remains that God—the Maker of
heaven and earth—created the nation of Israel through
His divinely spoken Word and therefore the blessing can
never be revoked or annulled. "I will make you a great
nation; I will bless you and make your name great" (v. 2).

Abraham was called to a new revelation of God's will
and rose to a level of faith that few have attained. God
spoke to Abraham as one speaks to a friend, face-to-face.
God took Abraham into His confidence, as well as into
His fellowship, and made a promise of personal blessing,
saying, "I will bless you." Genesis 13:2 records: "Abram
was very rich in livestock, in silver, and in gold." It was
a temporal earthly blessing, which was very personal. A
blessed man experiences good relationships in his marriage, with his children, and with his friends; he and his
family enjoy good health and healing; he gets promoted

at his place of employment. His house sells quickly while his neighbors wait for months without success. His business thrives when other businesses shrivel. All of these blessings are temporal and very personal.

Concerning a blessed man, people might say, "He has the Midas touch!" Wrong! Our power to prosper is made possible by God's faithfulness to His word through His Prophetic Blessing. That blessing is carried over to his wife, his children, his grandchildren, and everything he puts his hand to. Wherever he goes, whatever he does, succeeds. This is but a mere glimpse of the impact of God's Prophetic Blessing upon families as demonstrated in the Word of God.

The Prophetic Blessing is personal and is available to you, your children, and your grandchildren today!

GOD'S BLESSING OF JACOB

The parade of blessing continues as Abraham's son Isaac blessed Jacob. God performed a divine sonogram on the womb of Rebekah, who was concerned about the condition of her pregnancy and asked—as many expectant mothers have throughout recorded history—"If all is well, why am I like this?" (Genesis 25:22). The Almighty read the sonogram of the children in Rebekah's womb and gave this prophetic proclamation:

Two nations are in your womb, two peoples shall be separated from your body; one people shall be stronger than the other, and the older [Esau] shall serve the younger [Jacob]. (Genesis 25:23)

When God looked into Rebekah's womb, He did not see a blob of meaningless, lifeless flesh; He saw two living human beings. He gave a prophetic proclamation that Jacob and his descendants, the Jewish people, would be stronger than his brother, Esau, and his descendants. Jacob, the heel catcher, was a rascal who knew the power of the blessing and used his craft and cunning to deceptively obtain it from his aged father, Isaac. Esau foolishly relinquished his right to the blessing for a bowl of beans and suffered greatly for it.

God the Father knew Jacob's destiny, and He called it forth as He spoke a Prophetic Blessing over him:

Then God appeared to Jacob again . . . and blessed

him. And God said to him, "Your name is Jacob; your name shall not be called Jacob anymore, but Israel shall be your name." So He called his name Israel. Also God said to him: "I am God Almighty. Be fruitful and multiply; a nation and a company of nations shall proceed from you, and kings shall come for your body. The land which I gave Abraham and Isaac I give to you; and to your descendants after you I give this land." (Genesis 35:9-12)

GOD'S BLESSING OF JEREMIAH

Even before he was born, Jeremiah, the weeping prophet, was known to God as a person with a specific destiny. Here is God's prophetic proclamation concerning Jeremiah's sonogram:

Then the word of the LORD came to me, saying: "Before I formed you in the womb I knew you; Before you were born I sanctified you; I ordained you a prophet to the nations." (Jeremiah 1:4-5)

This verse clearly declares three things:

1. God knew your child before he or she was conceived in the womb.

2. God has called children to a divine work and has sanctified them for that work while they were in their mother's womb.

3. God has ordained your children's divine destiny.

GOD'S BLESSING OF JOHN THE BAPTIST

Zacharias was an elderly priest in Israel who was married to a woman named Elizabeth. They had no children because Elizabeth was barren, and they were both well advanced in years. Zacharias went to the temple to serve his rotation, as was the custom of the priesthood. While he was praying, the angel Gabriel appeared to him saying:

Do not be afraid, Zacharias, for your prayer is heard; and your wife Elizabeth will bear you a son, and you shall call his name John. And you will have joy and gladness, and many will rejoice at his birth. For he will be great in the sight of the Lord, and shall drink neither wine nor strong drink. He will also be filled with the

Holy Spirit, even from his mother's womb. And he will turn many of the children of Israel to the Lord their God. He will also go before Him in the spirit and power of Elijah, "to turn the hearts of the fathers to the children," and the disobedient to the wisdom of the just, to make ready a people prepared for the Lord. (Luke 1:13–17)

The angel of the Lord gave Zacharias the exact details about the life and future ministry of the child in the womb of Elizabeth. The angel also declared that John the Baptist would be filled with the Holy Spirit in the womb of his mother. Only a human being can have a supernatural experience, not a blob of flesh. Diana and I are the proud parents of five wonderful children and grandparents to twelve amazing grandchildren, who are all the joy of our lives. We can undeniably state that they are God's greatest blessing to us.

THE PROPHETIC BLESSINGS FROM JESUS CHRIST

The blessing continued in the New Testament with a Jewish rabbi, Jesus of Nazareth, as He sat on a rock by the Sea of Galilee. Christ revealed to the multitudes the foundational principles of our faith through what has become known as the Sermon on the Mount, which includes eight Prophetic Blessings known as the Beatitudes.

These Prophetic Blessings—spoken from the mouth of the Son of God, our ultimate spiritual authority—are meant for every person on earth. These blessings have the power to resurrect your dead marriage, bring you supernatural joy, provide you peace of mind, create healthy self-esteem, and help establish an unshakable foundation for enduring life's greatest storms. From time to time, Jesus even paused from teaching the multitudes to bless the children. The Gospel of St. Mark records: "He took them up in His arms, laid His hands on them, and blessed them" (10:16).

What did He say? He said what rabbis and Jewish fathers have been saying for thousands of years: "The LORD make His face shine upon you, and be gracious to you; the LORD lift up His countenance upon you, and give you peace" (Numbers 6:25–26). And then, as spiritual authorities, Jesus and Jewish fathers spoke into existence the future their spiritual eyes could see for the children. This is the power of the Prophetic Blessing. If

Jesus took time to bless the children, why don't we?

The last picture we have of Jesus in Scripture is on the Mount of Transfiguration saying farewell to His disciples. As He rose into the heavens, He looked down on His devoted followers and blessed them. The Gospel of St. Luke records: "And He led them out as far as Bethany, and He lifted up His hands and blessed them. Now it came to pass, while He blessed them, that He was parted from them and carried up into heaven" (24:50–51).

God blessed Abraham, Isaac, Jacob, and Jacob's twelve sons, who served Him with their hearts and lives in the Old Testament through the fulfillment of the Prophetic Blessing they received. Jesus Christ blessed His followers in the New Testament with eight Prophetic Blessings imparted on a mountainside in Galilee, blessings that transformed their lives and created the blueprint for the future of Christianity. Now God desires to bless you and your children as you commit your life to do His will and release the power of the Prophetic Blessing into your family!

CHAPTER 3

RELEASING THE *Blessing* THROUGH THE SPOKEN WORD

In order to make the blessings of God a reality in your life and in the lives of your children and grandchildren, you must release the God-ordained Prophetic Blessing over them through the Spoken Word. God wants to bless your children, but you must take action in order to release the blessing and for them to receive the blessing in their lives. Scripture reminds us that we must do our part. We cannot receive without asking, we cannot open a door without knocking, we cannot find without seeking. In the same way, we cannot bless without first releasing the blessings according to the Spoken Word of God.

THE POWER OF THE SPOKEN WORD

Your speech is a gift from God. Man is the only creature with the God-given power to communicate through words. Words are a transcript of your mind, a reflection of your heart, and when you use them, they paint a picture of your soul. Like most paintings, words can be inspiringly beautiful or downright ugly! Jesus was very aware of what our words reveal, for He said, "Out of the abundance of the heart the mouth speaks" (Matthew 12:34).

Words have the power to bring comfort and healing or hurt and destruction. Every person reading this book knows someone whose life has been enhanced or poisoned by the power of words. The power of life and death are found in the tongue. Solomon wrote in Proverbs 18:21, "Death and life are in the power of the tongue, and those who love it will eat its fruit."

Notice the extreme choices God offers in this verse: *death* or *life*—nothing in between. There is no middle ground; everything that comes out of your mouth produces hope or despair, a blessing or a curse, life or death. James continued in his epistle, "If anyone among you thinks he is religious, and does not bridle his tongue but deceives his own heart, this one's religion is useless" (James 1:26).

Here are a few pearls of wisdom you should file away in your brain bank. They will help you lead a successful life:

- It does not require many words to speak the truth.[1]
- Words can make a deeper scar than silence can ever heal.[2]
- Kind words are short to speak, but their echoes are endless.[3]

THE POWER OF WORDS IN CREATION

The statement "God said . . ." occurs ten times in the first chapter of Genesis, establishing the power of the Spoken Word. With one statement, God removed the force of darkness over the earth. He said, "Let there be light," and the marvelous and mysterious power of light was born. No one can tell us what light is, only what it does. It is one of the most mysterious elements in the universe. Men have attempted to harness light and, with their effort, have convoluted its purpose, for light has become a new absolute in physics and is the core of $E=mc^2$, a formula that ushered in the atomic age.[4]

God continued to create the universe with the supernatural power of prophetic speech. "*Then God said, 'Let there be a firmament in the midst of the waters, and let it divide the waters from the waters'*" (Genesis 1:6). Through the supernatural power of words, God separated the clouds from the waters of the sea. Not an easy task, my friends, for water is 773 times the weight of air, and there is suspended in the air above the oceans of the world an estimated 54.5 trillion tons of vapor.[5] Finally, a number that is higher than our national debt!

"*Then God said, '*Let the earth bring forth grass, the herb that yields seed, and the fruit tree that yields fruit according to its kind' . . . and it was so" (Genesis 1:11). Nature in all its splendor was created by the power of God's words. It is important to notice how Moses classified plant life because "botanists use a similar division dividing plants into *acotylidons*, the seedless plants, *monocotylidons*, the seed-bearing plants and *dicotylidons*, the fruit-bearing plants. This system of classification, the fruit of centuries of research, is still used to this day and was written by Moses onto the Bible's very first page."[6]

"*Then God said*, 'Let there be lights in the firmament of the heavens to divide the day from the night; and let them be for signs and seasons, and for days and years; and let them be for lights in the firmament of the heavens to give light on the earth'; and it was so. Then God made two great lights: the greater light to rule the day, and the lesser light to rule the night. He made the stars also" (Genesis 1:14–16).

To create our vast universe, God had only to speak—and it was so.

WORD AND SPIRIT WORKING TOGETHER

In his book *The Power of Proclamation*, Derek Prince introduced the concept of the written Word of God and the Spirit of God working together to produce the power of the Spoken Word. For instance, when God created man, He said, "Let Us make man in Our [God and Jesus'] image, according to Our likeness" (Genesis 1:26). In the next chapter, the Word says, "And the LORD God formed man of the dust of the ground, and breathed into his nostrils the breath of life; and man became a living being" (Genesis 2:7). Again, the Hebrew word for "breath" is *ruach*, meaning "spirit," and with respect to this verse in particular, *ruach* or *breath* is referring to the Spirit of God.[7]

In order to give Adam life, God literally breathed His own Spirit into him. King David spoke of this same creative power when he declared, "By the word of the LORD the heavens were made, and all the host of them by the breath of His mouth. . . . For He spoke, and it was done; He commanded, and it stood fast" (Psalm 33:6, 9).

It is the Word of God that performs the supernatural work, not man, for even Jesus said, "The Son can do nothing of Himself, unless it is something He sees the Father doing; for whatever the Father does, these things the Son also does in like manner" (John 5:19 NASB). We too pass on the Prophetic Blessing when we proclaim it with a believing heart and with believing lips.[8]

THE SPOKEN WORD IS PROPHETIC

Some may accept that the Spoken Word is powerful, but they will question the theological concept that the

Spoken Word is prophetic. Let's allow the guiding light of the Word of God to reveal the answer. Isaac blessed Jacob and Esau, and both blessings came true exactly as spoken. Jacob blessed his twelve sons and two grandsons, Manasseh and Ephraim. Those blessings came true exactly as spoken. Jesus blessed His twelve disciples, saying, "You are the salt of the earth" and "the light of the world" (Matthew 5:13–14).

At the time Jesus spoke this Prophetic Blessing over His disciples, they were saturated with serious character flaws. If Jesus had hired a Jerusalem management firm to give Him an evaluation of the emotional profiles of His twelve disciples at the time He proclaimed the blessing over their lives, it would have read as follows:

Dear Jesus of Nazareth,

Thank You for entrusting our firm to perform the psychological profiles on the men You have selected to lead Your ministry. After careful evaluation, we have come to the following conclusions: Simon Peter exhibits bipolar tendencies. If incited, his behavior may culminate in fits of rage inflicting harm on others. James and

John are highly competitive and self-centered and will most likely attempt a hostile takeover of Your organization. Thomas is self-doubting, uncertain, and lacks confidence, while Matthew has been barred from the Merchant Men's Fellowship of Greater Jerusalem. Upon close examination, we have determined that if You do not reconsider these choices, Your ministerial vision to evangelize the world will not succeed.

Despite these flaws, Jesus looked at His twelve ragged, basically uneducated, imperfect followers and spoke this blessing over them: "You are the salt of the earth ... [and] the light of the world" (Matthew 5:13–14).

They received Christ's blessing in faith and acted upon it. At that exact moment they were nothing, but they rose to the level of accomplishment spoken by Jesus in His Prophetic Blessing, and they went out and shook the world.

THE SUPERNATURAL POWER OF JESUS' SPEECH

When Jesus and His disciples were crossing the Sea of Galilee, the winds became contrary to the point that the disciples—some of whom were professional fishermen—were terrified, thinking they would surely die. The frightened disciples awakened Jesus, shouting above the howling winds and waves pounding the boat: "'Do You not care that we are perishing?' Then He arose and rebuked the wind, and said to the sea, 'Peace, be still!' And the wind ceased and there was a great calm" (Mark 4:38–39). Jesus spoke . . . and it was so!

Jesus stood before the tomb of Lazarus four days after his death and simply spoke: "'Lazarus, come forth!' And he who had died came out" (John 11:43–44). Jesus spoke . . . and it was so! Lepers were forced to live outside the city in an isolated colony until death mercifully ended their grueling suffering. However, one leper managed to get to Jesus and make a simple statement: "Lord, if You are willing, You can make me clean." Jesus responded, "I am willing; be cleansed" (Luke 5:12–13). Jesus spoke . . . and it was so! This voice that calmed the sea, raised the dead, and cured the leper was the same voice that spoke to the darkness on Creation morning, and darkness fled from the face of the earth.

I can read your mind right now. You're saying, "Pastor Hagee, everyone knows the speech of God and that of Jesus, His Son, is supernatural . . . but mine isn't!" Wrong! Your speech unleashes God's power anytime you proclaim the Word of God.

Every time Derek Prince took the pulpit, he spoke about God's Word and its power to heal the sick, deliver the oppressed, and redeem the lost. Derek met His Savior face-to-face several years ago, and I miss him dearly; however, he left with me—and millions of other believers—teachings that are engraved on our hearts for eternity. I will never forget the beautiful word picture he painted when he spoke on the infinite power of God's Word. Allow me to share a portion of his inspirational message with you: Every Bible-believing Christian has a rod in his hand—the Word of God. Think of your Bible as the only instrument you need in your hand to be able to do everything God calls you to do.

The first thing you need to realize is the power of God's Word. It is a supernatural book. Just like Moses' rod, the Bible contains power. This isn't obvious when you first look at it, but when you understand it, the power is actually limitless.[9] It is crucial for you to comprehend how powerful your words can be to revolutionize your life, your marriage, your children, and your business, as well as to literally reshape your future.

Whenever the words we say with our mouths agree with the Word of God, Jesus, the "High Priest of our confession," will release His authority and His blessing from heaven on our words here on earth (Hebrews 3:1). You have unbelievable supernatural power through your divinely directed speech.

GOD'S BLESSING ON MATTHEW

When I sit on the platform of Cornerstone Church and watch our son Matthew preaching to our congregation and our television audience that reaches across the nation and around the world, it's all I can do to keep myself from jumping to my feet and shouting for joy. He is an answer to prayer—and Satan tried to kill him while he was in his mother's womb.

Diana and I were thrilled when the doctor confirmed

she was pregnant with Matthew. A few weeks after the news of her pregnancy, Diana ministered to a young girl in our church who was not feeling well. The following day the girl's mother called to inform Diana that the doctor had diagnosed her daughter's condition over the phone as German measles.

When Diana called her obstetrician to report that she had been exposed to German measles, he reviewed Diana's records and concluded that she had never had the measles nor had she ever received the immunization against the virus. The doctor proceeded to inform Diana that the German measles, medically known as rubella, can cause deformity and severe brain damage to a child in the mother's womb.

Diana was in shock but was somewhat relieved when she heard her doctor softly say, "Don't worry. We can take care of everything with one visit to the office." Diana asked what his plan for treatment was. His answer: "It's a simple in-office procedure called dilation and curettage, or a D&C. It's an easy procedure that can be done in less than an hour." In other words . . . an abortion!

Diana hung up the phone and turned pale as tears started streaming down her face. She had attended the university as a premed student and knew instantly we were in a crisis of faith.

Diana called my office, crying, as she related to me the doctor's plan to terminate her pregnancy. "What are we going to do?" she sobbed into the phone.

"Step one: fire the doctor! We're going to trust God that the life in your body will be born perfectly healthy and fulfill the divine destiny God has already charted!" I immediately called the doctor and dismissed him. Before we hung up, he gave me the "irresponsible person" speech, trying to manipulate me with guilt to terminate the pregnancy. He failed!

When Diana arrived at my office, her eyes were swollen from crying. She sat down in a chair across from my desk, looked me straight in the eye, and said, "Now what?"

What do you do when you don't know what to do? You do exactly this: "Trust in the LORD with all your heart, and lean not on your own understanding; *in all your ways* acknowledge Him, and He shall direct your paths" (Proverbs 3:5–6).

We cried in each other's arms, proclaimed a healthy pregnancy and delivery, and then waited on God.

Are you ready for this? Three days later, the woman who had called Diana to report that her daughter had German measles called again. She told Diana, "I wanted to follow up with you on the condition of our daughter. She began to improve much quicker than the doctor had predicted, so I took her into his office where he confirmed that he had misdiagnosed her. It was only a skin rash of some kind, not the German measles."

Diana began to weep again, out of gratitude and relief, but also out of anguish as her mind fell on the unthinkable: had we followed the advice of our doctor, Matthew never would have been born.

Matthew's birth was the first of our children's that the hospital allowed me to witness. I saw him take his first breath. I was the first to hold him. As I held our healthy miracle baby in my arms, he smiled his first smile, and I wept for joy. Had Matthew's life been taken in his mother's womb, the Lord's divine destiny for him would have been aborted as well.

I am the fifth consecutive generation in the Hagee family to become a pastor; our son Matthew continues this revered heritage as the sixth generation to preach the gospel of Jesus Christ. Diana and I are praying that one of his sons will continue the legacy of the Hagee family.

I thank You, Lord, for the revelatory truth of Your precious Word: "I have come that they may have life, and that they may have it more abundantly" (John 10:10).

THE SPOKEN WORD IS A WEAPON OF WARFARE

The Bible again paints a picture of the Spoken Word in Ephesians 6 through the teaching on the armor of God:

Therefore take up the whole armor of God, that you may be able to withstand in the evil day, and having done all, to stand. . . . And take the helmet of salvation, and the sword of the Spirit, which is the word of God; praying always with all prayer and supplication in the Spirit, being watchful to this end with all perseverance and supplication for all the saints—and for me, that utterance may be given to me, that I may open my mouth boldly to make known the mystery of

the gospel, for which I am an ambassador in chains;
that in it I may speak boldly, as I ought to speak.
(vv. 13, 17–20)

In this passage the "sword" refers to the actual Word of God (see Revelation 1:16 KJV—"out of His mouth went a sharp two-edged sword"). And the "Spirit" is the *breath* or *ruach* of God, which I explained earlier in this chapter.

So, in commanding us to arm ourselves with "the sword of the Spirit," Paul was not telling us to fight "against the wiles of the devil" by throwing our fourteen-pound Bible at him (Ephesians 6:11). No! These verses command us to fight the devil by boldly opening our mouths and literally *speaking* the Word of God.

I cannot say this often enough: Christians must realize that the Spoken Word is an instrument of authority given to us by God to release His power into every area of our lives. The Spoken Word can be used to bless, and it can also be used as a weapon of spiritual warfare against the powers and principalities of darkness.

Scripture records the advantage that can be had through the Spoken Word during such warfare:

Let the saints be joyful in glory;
Let them sing aloud on their beds.
Let the high praises of God be in their mouth,
And a two-edged sword in their hand,
To execute vengeance on the nations,
And punishments on the peoples;
To bind their kings with chains,
And their nobles with fetters of iron;
To execute on them the written judgment—
This honor have all His saints.
Praise the LORD! (Psalm 149:5–9)

The psalmist is clearly describing spiritual warfare! But more importantly, he is revealing the awesome power that the Spoken Word has over our enemies.

The power of the Spoken Word gives the believer the authority to proclaim the promises within the Bible, and one of those promises is victory: "For the LORD your God is the one who goes with you to fight for you against your enemies to give you victory" (Deuteronomy 20:4 NIV).

However, unless these promises are spoken, they cannot fulfill their purpose. One must open his or her mouth and proclaim the "written judgment" in order for the power stored within it to be released. Jesus Himself used the Spoken Word in spiritual battles.

In Matthew 4, we read about Satan tempting Jesus. The Holy Spirit led Jesus into the wilderness where, after Jesus had fasted for forty days, the devil began to tempt Him, saying, "If You are the Son of God, command that these stones become bread" (v. 3). Christ's instant response was "It is written, 'Man shall not live by bread alone, but by every word that proceeds from the mouth of God'" (v. 4). In total, Satan tempted Jesus three times, and each time Jesus fought back by opening His mouth and proclaiming the Scriptures.

God was the Word and the Word was God, yet even Jesus, in all of His majesty and power, spoke the Word in a time of spiritual warfare! There is no mystery concerning the victor in this fight:

> *Jesus said to him, "Away with you, Satan! For it is written, 'You shall worship the LORD your God, and Him only you shall serve.'" Then the devil left Him, and behold, angels came and ministered to Him. (Matthew 4:10–11)*

Jesus faced spiritual warfare, and so will you. That is guaranteed. You can't avoid the battle, but you can be equipped to win it. God has declared that you have His powerful Word as part of your armor to shield you from the enemy's attack. This is a revolutionary thought for many of you. Would you go into battle without your helmet or bulletproof vest? Not unless you want to die shortly after the battle begins.

EVA'S STORY

I heard this powerful testimony from members of our Cornerstone family. It beautifully illustrates the power of the Spoken Word in spiritual warfare.

My husband and I were thrilled when we learned that we were expecting our second child. We knew in our hearts that this baby was a little girl long before her sex was confirmed. Our first child was a beautiful boy named Elijah, so we decided to name our little girl Elisha.

I was shocked when the doctor announced at my first visit that the sonogram showed no heartbeat. The doctor said, "I would normally prescribe a D&C, but I'm going to wait two more weeks before I perform the procedure."

Devastated, I went home to my prayer closet for a time of extended prayer. Two weeks passed and I anxiously went back to the doctor, where he joyfully proclaimed that I had a healthy baby growing within me! He announced, "This little one has a purpose!" I knew he was right!

From that moment on I prayed over my unborn baby, calling her by the name we had chosen, Elisha. One morning while I was in my prayer closet, I heard the Lord speak to my spirit, saying, "You shall name this child *Eva*, for the name means 'life.' There will be many days the enemy will come to speak death, but you will counter the enemy's efforts every time you speak her name!"

I had no idea what that statement would mean and the power it would hold in the immediate future of our little girl.

When Eva was born, the umbilical cord was wrapped so tightly around her neck that the doctor had to rip the cord in two to ensure her safe delivery.

Still in her infancy, Eva had an unusual allergic reaction that threatened her life. As we rushed her to the hospital, we passionately called out her name and cried, declaring, "The Lord said you shall live and not die!" God miraculously touched our daughter once again.

When Eva was two years of age, she experienced yet another life-threatening crisis. We were out of town and received the terrible call that Eva had accidentally fallen fifteen feet out of a second-story window while under a sitter's care. When I received the horrible news that Eva had split her head from front to back and her bottom lip had detached from her jawbone, my head reeled and my heart sank. Yet I kept proclaiming aloud, "God has promised that she would live and not die!"

As my baby lay in the trauma unit covered in her blood, I stood over her and softly spoke her name. I would say, "Eva, your name means 'life.' Mommy and Daddy declared it from day one, and we believe what God has said is truth!"

We have just celebrated three years since her supernatural recovery from that life-threatening fall. At the age of five, Eva is beautiful, robustly healthy, and full of life.

In the many times that Eva's life was in peril, her father and I cried out to God and spoke things that were not as though they were. Every time we called Eva by name . . . we spoke life! We thank God every day that we listened to His voice and obeyed His instruction to name our precious daughter Eva; for God is truly the Giver of life! She is alive today because of the divine power of God's Word.

There is no reason for you, my friend, to lose the battle you are currently fighting. Go to the Word. Read it with faith. Then in faith believe it, in faith declare it, and watch your mountains of impossibility begin to disappear!

Listen and believe the Words of Jesus: "For assuredly, I say to you, if you have faith as a mustard seed, you will say to this mountain, 'Move from here to there,' and it will move; and *nothing will be impossible for you"* *(Matthew 17:20).*

PROCLAIMING THE PROPHETIC BLESSING

The verb *to proclaim* comes from the Latin meaning "to shout forth." A biblical proclamation is an official declaration of God's Word over the life of the believer. Scripture says we are to proclaim the praises of God:

> *You are a chosen generation, a royal priesthood, a holy nation, His own special people, that you may proclaim the praises of Him who called you out of darkness into His marvelous light. (1 Peter 2:9)*

Every proclamation should be based upon one or more Scriptures that apply to your specific need. On one occasion when my dear friend Rabbi Scheinberg and I were discussing the Torah, he passionately described his love for the Word: "I believe that the Word is God and God is the Word. I believe that the *Shekinah* [the Holy Spirit] abides between the Hebrew letters of the written Word, and as the letters leap upward, they are like the cloven tongues of fire giving the Word life! I believe that the Word is dynamic [alive and powerful], which is why the believer can read a Scripture verse one day and it mean one thing and read the same verse another day and it means another!"

After you have defined your specific circumstance, allow the Holy Spirit to reveal the Scriptures that will empower you to receive your blessing. Once you have identified them, begin to proclaim God's promises over your life. There is a miracle in your mouth activated by the living Word of God. King David wrote, "Hear my prayer, O God; give ear to the words of my mouth" (Psalm 54:2) and "I cried out to him with my mouth; his praise was on my tongue" (Psalm 66:17 NIV). Proceed from reading the Scripture aloud to systematic memorization of the Word. King David declared, "Your word I have hidden in my heart, that I might not sin against You" (Psalm 119:11). The phrase *hidden in my heart* means "to memorize." The Hebrew expression *to learn by heart* is to learn by *mouth*.

Torah-believing Jews begin their morning prayers by putting on their *tallit* (prayer shawl) and strapping their *tefillin*/phylacteries (small boxes that contain parchment scrolls of Scripture) on their left hand and their head as they proclaim the Word of God. The writings placed within these boxes are Exodus 13:1–16 and Deuteronomy 6:4–9, 13–21. This is what Deuteronomy 6:4–9 proclaims:

> *Hear, O Israel: The LORD our God, the LORD is one!*
>
> *You shall love the LORD your God with all your heart, with all your soul, and with all your strength.*
>
> *And these words which I command you today shall be in your heart. You shall teach them diligently to your children, and shall talk of them when you sit in your house, when you walk by the way, when you lie down, and when you rise up. You shall bind them as a sign on your hand, and they shall be as frontlets between your eyes. You shall write them on the doorposts of your house and on your gates.*

Some Jewish sages believe that "the wearing of tefillin is one commandment that even God observes."[10] Imagine it! Jesus, a rabbi who lived by the law of Moses, put on His prayer shawl and placed the tefillin on His hand and head every morning before prayer as He quoted the prophet Hosea:

> *I will betroth you to Me forever;*
> *Yes, I will betroth you to Me*
> *In righteousness and justice,*
> *In lovingkindness and mercy;*
> *I will betroth you to Me in faithfulness,*
> *And you shall know the LORD (2:19–20).*

If the Son of God considered proclaiming the Word crucial to His daily ministry, how much more should we?

If you refuse to proclaim God's Word over your life and the lives of your loved ones through the Prophetic Blessing, you cut yourself off from your High Priest in heaven. God can only get involved in your life and in your dreams for the future when you call out to Him in prayer. The initiative rests with *you*. The Bible says, "Whatever you bind on earth will be bound in heaven, and whatever you loose on earth will be loosed in heaven" (Matthew 16:19). God is waiting to hear from you before He will release His power to enforce your divine speech.

> *The word is near you, in your mouth and in your heart" (that is, the word of faith which we preach): that if you confess with your mouth the Lord Jesus and believe in your heart that God has raised Him from the dead, you will be saved. For with the heart one believes unto righteousness, and with the mouth confession is made unto salvation. (Romans 10:8–10)*

CHAPTER 4

RELEASING THE *Blessing* THROUGH PHYSICAL TOUCH

People often lament that the blessings of God are not evident in their lives. They believe that the Prophetic Blessing established in the Bible is either an inaccessible prize or something that God capriciously imparts based on the recipients' good deeds. Fortunately for us, and through the goodness of our Creator, we *are* able to release His blessings in our lives, positively impacting our marriages and our relationships with our children and grandchildren as well as experiencing the unlimited favor of God. Christ did it; why can't we?

While here on earth, Christ healed and blessed those around Him through the touch of His hands and the power of His prophetic proclamations. We too have the power of touch when linked to God's Spoken Word! That there is power in human touch is not a new concept, nor is it an exclusively religious one.

PHYSICAL TOUCH HAS HEALING POWER

Science has proven that touch, in and of itself, has healing power. As multiple miracles in the Bible have shown that touch has the power to bless and heal, so medical science has proven that touch not only can heal but also has the power to keep you in good mental and emotional health—two of God's greatest blessings.

Dr. Tiffany Field, founder of the Touch Research Institute at the University of Miami School of Medicine, spoke of the restorative power of touch, saying it yields "specific effects, such as reduced pain for those with arthritis, increased peak air flow for those with asthma, and increased natural killer cell activity for the HIV patient."[1]

Furthermore, scientific studies have shown that children may actually die from lack of physical touch.

In a study from the early twentieth century, mortality rates of children who lived in institutional facilities, specifically orphanages and foundling homes, were compared to those of children who had been neglected by their parents.[2] The obvious thought was that, as a result of providing for the children's physical needs, the facilities would have a lower mortality rate than the group of children whose parents had abandoned them. Astoundingly, the results showed no difference between the mortality rates of neglected children in families and children in orphanages. Although the institutions met the children's physical requirements, such as food, clothing, and shelter, "as many children died as survived" with this institutionalized care.[3]

More specifically, a study of American orphanages in 1915 found the mortality rate for children younger than the age of two was between 32 percent and 75 percent, with certain hospitals in Baltimore and New York reaching mortality rates of approximately 90 percent and nearly 100 percent, respectively.[4] Yet, despite this study, roughly fifteen years would pass before these disturbing mortality rates would be attributed to the lack of physical touch. The children in these facilities were not touched due to their caretakers' indifference and because societal norms at the time prohibited it. In the late nineteenth and early twentieth centuries, nurturing contact between caretakers and children at these institutions was uncommon, if not forbidden.[5]

However, in the late 1920s, in an attempt to determine the healing effects of touch, those caring for babies in New York's Bellevue Hospital were required to include physical touch in the daily care of their pediatric patients. Surprisingly, after the hospital incorporated physical nurturing contact into their treatment plans, the mortality rates of the hospitalized children decreased by over 20 percent.[6] Thereafter, physical contact between caregiver and child became the rule rather than the exception. Once this practice was integrated into orphanages, the mortality rates of children in these facilities plummeted.[7]

HE TOUCHED ME

As important as this study was to the scientific discovery of "touch deprivation" versus the positive impact of touch, one could have reached the same conclusion by reading the Word of God: we can see that Christ set a similar example. Matthew 19:13–15 reads:

> *Then little children were brought to Him that He might put His hands on them and pray, but the disciples rebuked them. But Jesus said, "Let the little children come to Me, and do not forbid them; for of such is the kingdom of heaven." And He laid His hands on them and departed from there.*

In their work *The Gift of the Blessing*, Gary Smalley and John Trent point out that in laying His hands on the children, Jesus was not only trying to teach the crowd a "spiritual lesson," but, in touching them, He was also meeting the actual needs of the children themselves.[8] The authors discuss that if Christ's objective were solely to teach, He would have merely used the children as an object in His lesson, as He did in Matthew 18. There, when asked by the disciples, "Who then is greatest in the kingdom of heaven?" Jesus responded by calling a child over to Him, setting that child "in the midst of them," and teaching that unless people convert and become as "little children," they will not enter the kingdom of heaven (vv. 1–3). However, in Matthew 19, not only did Christ teach a spiritual lesson, but He also met the physical, emotional, and spiritual needs of the children. Christ, in His perfect wisdom, "demonstrated His knowledge of a child's genuine need": He touched them.[9]

In addition to meeting their physical needs, by placing His hands on these children, Christ was also reiterating the importance of touch in the Hebrew tradition of releasing the blessing on our children. One need look no further than Genesis 27—and the "lengths to which Jacob and his mother went to have Isaac's hands of blessing laid on Jacob's head"[10]—to realize the significance of touch with respect to receiving the divine blessing of God.

SANDY'S STORY

I remember the life-and-death crisis Diana and I faced with our youngest daughter, Sandy, within hours after her birth. Even though Diana delivered Sandy three and a half weeks before her due date, all seemed perfect at first. Sandy was beautiful and, more importantly, apparently healthy! After holding our new baby daughter for several hours, Diana and I thanked the Lord for His goodness. I kissed them both good-bye and left the hospital to care for the other four children who were waiting at home. Life could not have been better!

As Diana held Sandy, she examined every detail of our new little girl. When the neonatal nurse came to take Sandy back to the nursery, Diana informed her of the purring sound coming from our precious baby every time she took a breath. The nurse made a note and wheeled Sandy out of the room. Diana called me to say good night, and we once again prayed a prayer of thanksgiving for the many blessings God had given us.

Several hours passed before Diana was awakened by three specialists who came into her room for a consultation. They stood by her bed and shared their grim prognosis: "We have examined your baby and found that her lungs are not functioning properly. After initial blood work, we feel she may have an infection in her bloodstream that may be life threatening. We need your permission to do further testing."

Diana was numb. She quickly signed the papers allowing the doctors to perform a myriad of additional tests on our tiny baby. Then Diana called me. I was awakened well after midnight from a deep and peaceful sleep by the clamoring ring of the telephone—never a good sign in the home of a pastor.

Diana began to tearfully relate what the doctors had said. After I consoled my wife with the promises of God, we united in prayer for our daughter. I told Diana I would be at the hospital as soon as the sitter came the next day to care for our other children. I never went back to sleep; instead I prayed until daybreak.

I hurried to the hospital early the next morning and found that Diana was not in her room. I rushed to the nurses' station, and they directed me to the neonatal unit, where I found Diana's swollen eyes staring into a plastic container that held our baby. The last time I had seen Sandy, she was in her mother's arms, swaddled in a pink blanket with her radiant, thick, black hair showing under her pink stocking cap. Now she was attached to what seemed like every wire imaginable and connected to a battery of monitors. Her little chest heaved up and down as she struggled for every breath. I looked into Diana's eyes and saw a distraught mother watching her baby fight for her life. Tears streamed down my face. I held my wife and whispered, "Lord, God of Abraham, Isaac, and Jacob, help us!"

We sat together staring at our precious gift of life and feeling helpless. Suddenly a nurse approached us and said, "Don't be afraid to touch your baby. Please make sure you are sanitized, and then you can place your hands in the incubator and let her know you are here." Diana and I were both relieved that we could show our new baby that we were there for her.

We both washed our hands thoroughly and donned special sterilized gowns, gloves, caps, and shoe covers. I approached the plastic container that was holding our treasure. The nurse opened the incubator door, and I remember placing my massive hand on her tiny, heaving chest, fearing I could somehow harm her. I cried out, "Lord, I ask that You heal my baby. Give her the fighting spirit to overcome this battle. I choose life over death and blessings for her life now and forevermore. Father, direct earthly physicians and bring healing to our baby."

From that moment, we never left Sandy's side. Diana and I touched her little body at every given opportunity. We sang to her, told her we loved her, and prayed for her without ceasing. In fact, Diana's obstetrician wanted to release her on the third day after Sandy's birth. Diana passionately refused to leave the hospital, stating, "I am not leaving this hospital without my baby!" The wise doctor changed his mind.

Our baby Sandy's little body endured six straight days of invasive testing. On the seventh day the doctors met with us to once again present their findings. I sat next to Diana and tightly held her hand as the doctors walked into our room, taking their seats in front of Diana's bed. Our hearts pounded as we waited to hear their results.

The head neonatologist took our breath away with his first words: "We don't know quite how to tell you, but . . ." He paused for what seemed an eternity. "Shortly after your baby's birth, she developed breathing problems as well as an infection in her blood. However, after thoroughly testing your baby, we find that she no longer shows any signs of either problem. I don't believe we made an initial misdiagnosis. All we can say is that she is healthy and ready to go home."

"Healthy and ready to go home!" That is what we heard—and it was music from heaven. Diana already had her bag packed. We could not leave the hospital quickly enough. We were so thankful to God for hearing our prayers and healing Sandy.

We waited for the nurse to bring her to us—and realized it was the same nurse who had given us permission to touch Sandy when she was battling for her little life. We thanked the nurse profusely for her encouragement. She shared our excitement about our good news and explained that she had cared for babies born with minor problems who had no one to love them or touch them and that, for no medical reason, they just slowly gave up their will to live and died. She informed us that the hospital had initiated a grandparent program where older volunteers would come and hold sick little babies and love them until they were out of danger. The power of a loving touch has the power of life!

The power of the Prophetic Blessing also endures. I had prayed that Sandy be given a "fighting spirit" to win her battle, and that spoken blessing stands to this day. Sandy is now an attorney who uses that fighting spirit in her daily life. She has also had to call on that supernatural inner strength several times in the lives of her own children. The power of the spoken blessing prevails and overcomes!

YOU NEVER OUTGROW
YOUR NEED FOR TOUCH

The need for touch is not just a childlike trait, nor is it something we ever outgrow. Science has confirmed that whether you are an unborn child in your mother's womb or a centenarian in the latter years of life, your physical need for touch never ceases. The truth is, as you become older, your need for human touch increases.

While researching the scientific evidence with respect to the power of touch, I came across some facts that resonated with me on a personal level. In her book *Touch*, Tiffany Field has pointed out that the older people get, the more they want to be touched. But ironically, the older someone gets, the less opportunity there is to be touched by another. Whether it is due to losing a spouse, friends, or family to death or failing health, there are myriad reasons why one's increasing age leads to a decrease in the type of social exchanges that foster human touch and interaction.[11] In fact, research has shown that "sensory deficits" lead to a surplus of "senile traits" in elderly nursing home residents.[12] Conversely, those residents who received touch in the form of massage therapy, hugs, or even a simple squeeze of the arm displayed fewer senile traits.

VADA'S STORY

These truths hit particularly close to home for me. For years, I begged my widowed mother to move from her home in Channelview, Texas—where she lived with my father for most of their married life—to San Antonio, where I have lived for more than fifty years.

Despite my repeated requests for her to move to San Antonio, Mother refused to leave her home. Obligingly, I honored her wishes and made the most of the visits she and I had together. My mother was extremely independent. She continued to run the family business after my father died, and she was very successful. She was not concerned about living alone. In fact, Mother was a lover of her Second Amendment rights and was not afraid to use them. My brother and I had to remove the firing pin from the loaded gun she kept under her pillow for fear she would hurt herself or some unsuspecting visitor.

But, from one visit to the next, I noticed a difference

in my mother. While her body was sound and her health intact, there was a change in her. I did not know the source of the problem, but I knew something was amiss. After twenty years of respecting her desire to stay alone in her home, I realized that I would have to act against the wishes of my very strong-willed mother and bring her to my hometown. She had reached the mental state where she did not know whether she had eaten or not; she left the gas on the stove wide open without lighting the flame; and eventually she did not recognize her own children when they walked into the room.

Upon my mother's arrival in San Antonio, Diana and I met with the best doctors available in order to find out what was wrong with her. Was it Alzheimer's or dementia? Extensive medical evaluations determined that my mother was physically sound although very frail. Her heart was strong; her lungs were clear; and despite some common ancillary health issues, which most people encounter at ninety-two years of age, there was nothing wrong with her physical health per se.

So, what was the problem? In layman's terms, the doctors said that the lack of sufficient daily interaction with other people due to her living alone for so many years had had a deteriorating effect on her mind. She had a mild degree of dementia due simply to a lack of human contact. I was extremely frustrated with myself for not making my mother move earlier!

We found a superb facility less than a mile from my office so that I could visit her regularly. In addition to the aides at the care center, Diana hired wonderful caretakers to be with my mom twenty-four hours a day. We knew the facility was adequately staffed and had the finest nurses and doctors in the city, but we did not want my mother to face another moment alone.

Not only did I not want her to *be* alone and have any of her needs go unnoticed—I did not want her to *feel* alone. There are subtleties like a sigh that may signal a need or a moan that might indicate discomfort that are easy to miss when a nurse has to care for multiple people. No matter what happened, someone was always there to reassure Mother that she was not alone.

In addition to helping with her prescribed medical care, my mother's caregivers—whom we referred to as her "little angels"—also held her hand, patted her face, and massaged her body with soothing lotion from head to toe twice each day. They spoke to her lovingly and often, even when she did not respond verbally. Astounded, we began to realize that my mother's caregivers, initially hired to provide nothing more than companionship and our peace of mind, kept her "in touch" with life through their constant and loving interaction with her. When she moved to San Antonio, she was a gaunt reflection of her former self; within months her weight became once again "Hagee healthy." More so, many of the symptoms of dementia disappeared.

My mother desired to go to heaven more than my grandchildren want to go to Disney World, yet she graduated from hospice care three times in her last four years! The Lord had many opportunities to call my mother home. Mother made it known decades ago that she did not want us to ever prolong her life artificially, and we honored her wishes.

When difficult choices needed to be made, we simply chose life as we prayed for her. The Word of God clearly instructs, "I have set before you life and death, blessing and cursing; therefore choose life, that both you and your descendants may live" (Deuteronomy 30:19). And in every case God intervened and kept His Word as she amazed her doctors and defied the odds.

I admit, I did not expect my mother to become almost a centenarian, and I often wondered what the Lord had planned for her life. However, I am convinced that the *power of a loving touch* assisted in extending my mother's life.

I know God is too wise to make a mistake, and He is too loving to be unkind. So I thank the Lord for the extra time He allowed me to have with my mother, and I know that, if nothing else, she was my number-one prayer warrior. For that, I will be eternally grateful and forever indebted to my mother who, through the power of parental blessing, changed my life forever.

When I was a child, Mother would gather her sons for prayer every night, but Saturday night was always prayer in preparation for church on Sunday, where the Hagee family spent the entire day. Our Saturday night ritual was to listen to the Grand Ole Opry on the radio as we ate freshly made popcorn and drank sweet tea out of quart jars.

As the evening came to a close, we'd gather for prayer in our living room. Mom would place her hands on the heads of her children and pray the Prophetic

Blessing of God into our lives. I can still hear my mother's fervent prayers—she never doubted the power of the Spoken Word of God. As a child, I almost felt sorry for the devil when I heard this zealous prayer warrior in action. I was confident that he was trembling in the corners of hell, for Vada Hagee had a very personal relationship with Jesus Christ.

A loving and merciful God has certainly heard and answered her prayers all these many years. I am confident that without the Prophetic Blessings spoken over me by my mother, my life would look very different today—and not in a good way. I am so thankful that I was raised in a godly home and that, through her obedience to God, my mother fulfilled her role as spiritual authority over her children, blessing our lives in countless ways.

Thirty days short of her ninety-ninth birthday—on April 30, 2012—my mother and the Lord made final earthly arrangements. God sent His heavenly hosts to escort Vada Mildred Hagee through the gates of heaven into her glorious eternal home where she had longed to be for so many years. As she left the bondage of her frail earthly tent, her spirit proclaimed, "I have fought the good fight, I have finished the race, I have kept the faith" (2 Timothy 4:7). And with that, she entered heaven, leaving me and those who follow behind me with this mandate: "Be watchful in all things, endure afflictions, do the work of an evangelist, fulfill your ministry" (v. 5). I love you, Momma.

THE HIGH PRIEST OF THE HOME

Just as my mother had authority over her children, so my father had authority over our household. In fact, there is a parallel relationship between Christ as the head of the church and the father as the head of the Christian home. Jesus Christ is our High Priest. Just as the Levitical high priests of the Old Testament were the conduits between the children of Israel and God Almighty, so Jesus Christ came to earth to serve as our lifeline to the Father. Hebrews reads, "Seeing then that we have a great High Priest who has passed through the heavens, Jesus the Son of God . . ." (4:14).

Moreover, just as Jesus is the High Priest of His church, so fathers are the high priests of their households (Ephesians 5:23). Just as Christ laid His hands on earthly children, so should a father lovingly lay hands upon his children in order to release the power of the Prophetic Blessing into their lives.

In the book of Numbers, the Lord gave specific instructions with respect to blessing the children of Israel. He instructed Moses to have Aaron, their high priest, bless the children of Israel by reciting the Priestly Blessing:

> *The LORD bless you and keep you;*
> *The LORD make His face shine upon you,*
> *And be gracious to you;*
> *The LORD lift up His countenance upon you,*
> *And give you peace. (Numbers 6:24–26)*

Then, in verse 27, the Lord continued: "So they shall put My name on the children of Israel, and I will bless them." In practice, not only did the priests bless the children of Israel by saying the name of God, but they literally took their fingers and traced the name of God upon the forehead or right hand of whomever they were blessing. In doing so, the priests were physically touching and putting God's name upon the children of Israel.[13]

This form of touching is so crucial that from the time of Moses until today, every Friday at sundown in Jewish homes around the world, fathers put their hands upon their children's heads and bless them with these very same words.

While the Jewish people are the physical descendants of Abraham, Christians are his spiritual descendants. Galatians 3:29 says, "If you are Christ's, then you are Abraham's seed, and heirs according to the promise." Therefore, Christian parents—as Abraham's seed—should place their hands upon their children and bless them as well.

Not only are parents to use touch to bless their children, but they should also use touch to train their children. The Word says, "Ye fathers, provoke not your children to wrath: but bring them up in the nurture and admonition of the Lord" (Ephesians 6:4 KJV). While we are all familiar with the biblical mandate to discipline our children, I fear some may overlook the mandate to "bring . . . up" their children. The Greek translation of the words *bring up* is *ektrepho*, which means "to nourish up to maturity" and "to nurture."[14]

Colossians 3:21 commands fathers not to "provoke

your children, lest they become discouraged." Accordingly, nurturing requires more than simply providing what is physically required for survival. To nurture one's children is to hug them, hold them in your arms, speak lovingly to them, encourage them, and kiss them on a daily basis.

Most importantly, whether you are disciplining your children or nurturing them, all of these acts should be carried out in love. After all is said and done, more is usually said than done. Love is not what you say; love is what you *do*!

THE TOUCH THAT BLESSES

What better way to show that you love your children than through tender, loving touch? Unfortunately, not only do some parents neglect to bless their children with words, but they also fail to touch them in meaningful ways. Notice again in the aforementioned Scripture from Ephesians that fathers are to "bring" or "nourish" their children "up to maturity." The point is that parents need to nourish their children in these meaningful ways until they are grown. Until—ideally—they find a spouse, who then assumes the role of nurturer.

So imperative is touch to the development of a child into an adult that research suggests physical violence in adolescence is the result of childhood touch deprivation.[15] A study conducted by Dr. J. H. Prescott "reported that most juvenile delinquents and criminals come from neglectful or abusive parents" and that "the deprivation of body touch, contact and movement are the basic causes of a number of emotional disturbances."[16] Central to Dr. Prescott's theory is that "lack of sensory stimulation in childhood leads to addiction to sensory stimulation in adulthood, resulting in delinquency, drug use and crime."[17]

This study was conducted in forty-nine comparable nonindustrial cultures around the globe. The only distinguishable differences in these otherwise similar cultures were that when children within a particular culture received minimal physical affection, that culture displayed high rates of adult violence. Conversely, when a culture displayed high levels of physical affection toward their children, there was no adult violence present.[18]

Dr. Prescott's study appears to be the Word of God on display and is an almost exact example of what happens in a culture when fathers provoke their children to wrath. It never ceases to amaze me when I see the truth of Scripture proven absolutely true in the crucible called life.

Despite the fact that touch has been shown to be a necessary component of healthy development, meaningful touch is practically prohibited in America's overly litigious society. A study conducted at the Touch Research Institute Nursery School found that, in spite of the school's name, its staff rarely touched its students. Fear of being accused of sexual abuse was the teachers' motivation in refraining from touching their students.[19]

How ironic that in today's "enlightened" society, we are so disoriented about what is appropriate for children. Some people have called for sex education to begin in kindergarten, yet at the same time our educators are afraid to give their students a reassuring pat on the back lest it be misinterpreted as sexual harassment.

Isn't it just like the enemy to take something that God has given us—such as the power of touch—and try to use it as a weapon against us? So, do not let the secular progressives take from us what God has blessed us with—the power of touch! God has blessed us in order that we may be a blessing. God has given us a mandate to lovingly touch others, and evidence of this is seen throughout the written Word: from God's creation of Adam and Eve in the garden (Genesis 2:7) to the command Christ gave to His church to touch ("*they will lay hands* on the sick, and they will recover" [Mark 16:18]).

As believers, we must touch in order to bless. Without loving touch, we are missing the mark in releasing the power of the Prophetic Blessing that we speak over our children, and our grandchildren, and future generations.

When is the last time you lovingly placed your hands on those you love and blessed them? Don't think about it . . . *do it!*

CHAPTER 5

HOW TO RELEASE THE PROPHETIC *Blessing* OVER YOUR CHILDREN

While it is inspirational to read or talk about the power of the Prophetic Blessing, it is better to actually declare it over your children and your grandchildren. Jewish fathers and mothers pray the blessing over their children every Sabbath. The blessing can be given by the mother or the father at any time of the day. Blessing your children each day before they leave for school or before they go to bed is a deed you will never regret and a blessing your children will never forget.

The other morning I quietly walked into my daughter Tina's home and saw her place her hands on the head of her daughter, Micah, before she left for a math competition. I overheard her utter the Prophetic

Blessing over her child. An even more beautiful sight was Micah reverently standing in front of her mother, eagerly receiving every word coming from the mouth of her spiritual authority.

Before my daughter and son-in-law, Sandy and Ryan, left on a recent trip, they gathered their two daughters, Olivia and Ellie, to pray a blessing of protection, peace, and joy over them. Sandy recounted that when Ryan was done, five-year-old Olivia began to weep. When they asked her why she was crying, she answered, "Daddy, your prayer made me feel so good. I am crying because I feel happy."

God is the source of every blessing, and He has chosen to release the Prophetic Blessing over your family through spiritual authority. God is ready and willing to open the windows of heaven and bless you with blessings you cannot possibly contain. "Every good gift [blessing] and every perfect gift is from above, and comes down from the Father of lights, with whom there is no variation or shadow of turning" (James 1:17).

As you prepare to speak God-ordained blessings over your children, let me give you an example of a time I spoke a Prophetic Blessing over one of my children.

MATTHEW'S STORY

When our son Matthew was about nine years of age, he said to his mother as she was tucking him into bed one Saturday night, "I need to talk to Daddy."

My wife has a curiosity factor that runs off the charts. Matt's "I need to talk to Daddy" statement brought a flurry of questions from his mother. "What do you need to talk to Daddy about? Is there a problem? Did you do something wrong? This is Saturday night; you know your daddy is lost in his study for tomorrow's sermon."

Matt stuck by his guns. "Momma, I need to talk to Daddy tonight—and I need to do it now!"

Diana came into my study with a very concerned look on her face and repeated Matthew's message. I asked, "What does he want to talk about?"

She responded, "He won't tell me; he said you are the only one he wants to talk to."

I closed my Bible, put my sermon notes in my briefcase, and walked up the stairs toward Matthew's bedroom. My mind was racing as I attempted to envision what had happened in Matthew's young life that made his request to specifically speak to me so urgent.

Of our five children, Matthew was always the most talkative and articulate. He was practically born talking. He started speaking whole sentences so early in life that adults found it entertaining to hold conversations with him even as a child.

I walked into his room, which was dimly lit by a small night-light beside his bed. I could see tears in his eyes, and my concern factor rocketed off the charts. *What had happened? What had he done?* I was comforted that he was too young to rob banks, take drugs, or chase girls. *What could a nine-year-old boy have done to move him to tears?*

I knelt beside his bed as tears ran down his cheeks. I melted like butter.

"What happened, Matt?"

"Daddy," he said with a trembling voice, "I've said something today that I feel has offended God."

"Would you like to talk about it?"

"No! I just want to make sure before I go to bed that God will forgive me, and if you ask Him, I know He will."

As I listened intently, I thought of the prophet Samuel, who as a child heard the voice of the Lord calling him when the high priest of Israel did not hear

God's voice. From the moment Matthew was born, Diana and I had prayed the double blessing over his life: "And so it was, when they had crossed over, that Elijah said to Elisha, 'Ask! What may I do for you, before I am taken away from you?' Elisha said, 'Please let a double portion of your spirit be upon me'" (2 Kings 2:9).

In an instant, this bedside chat went from just another talk with Daddy to a moment in time when the hand of God was shaping the future of a child . . . my child. I changed gears from counselor to the high priest of my house.

We asked God for forgiveness, and then I placed both my hands on Matt's head and prayed the Priestly Blessing over my son. Following the blessing, I asked the Lord to protect him from the forces of evil; to forgive his offenses; to provide him with good health; and to send angels before him and behind him to guide him all the days of his life.

I asked the Lord to bring Matthew into the service of God as a minister of the gospel and to bring him a godly wife and godly children who would forever be a source of joy in his life. We hugged tightly, and I walked out of his room only to bump into Diana, who was sitting at the top of the stairs. I recounted the story, and we held each other and cried, thanking God for our son, for his sensitivity to the Holy Spirit, and for his future.

Twenty-five years later, every word of that Prophetic Blessing has become reality.[1] Now's it's time to release this same supernatural power of the Prophetic Blessing over your children and grandchildren and then watch as God transforms their lives!

PREPARE TO RELEASE THE PROPHETIC BLESSING

First, prepare yourself by seeking the Lord in prayer. Then stand, extend your hands toward your loved one, and repeat the Priestly Blessing from Numbers 6:24–26 over him or her:

> *The LORD bless you and keep you;*
> *The LORD make His face shine upon you,*
> *And be gracious to you;*
> *The LORD lift up His countenance upon you,*
> *And give you peace.*

The next verse (Numbers 6:27) confirms that there is a divine order in the matter of releasing the supernatural power of the Prophetic Blessing: "So they [those in spiritual authority] shall put My name on the children of Israel." The word *so* makes it clear that the exact instructions God has given in the preceding text are to be carried out exactly in order to release His blessing.

Let's examine the six scriptural requirements for releasing and receiving the Prophetic Blessing as you prepare to proclaim aloud the Holy Spirit–directed Prophetic Blessing over your child's life.

SIX SCRIPTURAL REQUIREMENTS FOR RELEASING AND RECEIVING THE PROPHETIC BLESSING

1. The Prophetic Blessing is to be imparted by a person in spiritual authority.

The blessing belongs to God. He instructed Aaron and the priests to be His delegated spiritual authority: they were the pipeline through which the Prophetic Blessing flowed.

Speak to Aaron and his sons, saying, "This is the way you shall bless the children of Israel." (Numbers 6:23)

Aaron was the high priest of Israel, and his sons were of the tribe of Levi, which constituted the priesthood. They were the spiritual authority of the nation of Israel. Jesus Christ belonged to the tribe of Judah; He was not a Levite. Nonetheless, Christ became our High Priest, as Hebrews 7:14–17 records:

It is evident that our Lord arose from Judah, of which tribe Moses spoke nothing concerning priesthood. And it is yet far more evident if, in the likeness of Melchizedek, there arises another priest who has come, not according to the law of a fleshly commandment, but according to the power of an endless life. For He testifies:
"You are a priest forever
According to the order of Melchizedek."

The point of logic is that the Old Testament men of the tribe of Levi were priests by birth. The priesthood of the believer was passed to Jesus Christ by His death and resurrection on the cross as "a priest forever" (Psalm 110:4; Hebrews 7:17).

When a person becomes a believer in Jesus Christ, he is a "living stone," according to 1 Peter 2:5: "You also, as living stones, are being built up a spiritual house, a holy priesthood, to offer up spiritual sacrifices acceptable to God through Jesus Christ."

Every believer becomes a living stone at the moment of conversion. We are a holy priesthood, and later St. Peter called us a "royal priesthood" (1 Peter 2:9). Therefore, believers—both men and women—have the spiritual authority to release the blessing of God upon their children as well as receive the blessing from their own spiritual authority.

2. The Prophetic Blessing shall be given while standing.

In Scripture, *standing* is a sign of reverence and respect. Every priest stood when he ministered to the people. The people stood while Solomon dedicated the Temple. Jesus stands at the right hand of God.

> *At that time the LORD separated the tribe of Levi to bear the ark of the covenant of the LORD, to stand*

before the LORD to minister to Him and to bless in His name, to this day. *(Deuteronomy 10:8)*

Then the king turned around and blessed the whole assembly of Israel, while all the assembly of Israel was standing. *(2 Chronicles 6:3)*

[The Levites] shall be ministers in My sanctuary, as gatekeepers of the house and ministers of the house; they shall slay the burnt offering and the sacrifice for the people, and they shall stand before them to minister to them. *(Ezekiel 44:11)*

Then the LORD said to [Moses], "Take your sandals off your feet, for the place where you stand is holy ground." *(Acts 7:33)*

[Stephen], being full of the Holy Spirit, gazed into heaven and saw the glory of God, and Jesus standing at the right hand of God. *(Acts 7:55)*

In the US military, when an officer walks into the room, everyone of a lower rank stands in unison and salutes. I have had the honor of visiting many of the prime ministers of Israel, and when they walk into a room, everyone immediately stands to give tribute and show honor to the highest office in the land. When I read the scriptural text before I preach to the membership of Cornerstone Church, I call them to stand in honor of the Word of God.

Many reliable scriptural accounts confirm that one must stand when releasing the Prophetic Blessing, in reverence to God, who is ultimately bestowing the blessing upon His children through His Word.

3. When the delegated spiritual authority is speaking the Prophetic Blessing over someone, he or she does so with uplifted hands.

Then Aaron lifted his hand *toward the people, blessed them, and came down from offering the sin offering, the burnt offering, and peace offerings. (Leviticus 9:22)*

[Jesus] led [the disciples] out as far as Bethany, and He lifted up His hands *and blessed them. (Luke 24:50)*

Raised hands in Judaism are the physical portrait of the blessing, which contains fifteen words. Each of the fifteen words corresponds to a different part of the hand. The palm of the hand represents the last word (*shalom* or *peace*). "The spiritual authority who raises their hands with palms outward while praying alludes to the peace of God without which there can be no blessing."[2]

4. The Prophetic Blessing must be done in the name of the Lord.

So they shall put My name *on the children of Israel, and I will bless them. (Numbers 6:27)*

Then he may serve in the name of the LORD *his God as all his brethren the Levites do, who stand there before the LORD. (Deuteronomy 18:7)*

Then the priests, the sons of Levi, shall come near, for the LORD your God has chosen them to minister to Him and to bless in the name of the LORD. *(Deuteronomy 21:5)*

Whatever you do in word or deed, do all in the name of the Lord Jesus. *(Colossians 3:17)*

When invoking the blessing, *Kohanim* (the Levitical priests) literally place their hands on the forehead of the person receiving the Prophetic Blessing and trace the Hebrew name of the Lord with their fingertips.

God's recipe for spiritual revival in America is found in 2 Chronicles 7:14: "If My people who are called by *My name* will humble themselves, and pray and seek My face, and turn from their wicked ways, then will I hear from heaven, and will forgive their sin and will heal their land." Second Chronicles 6:6 states, "I have chosen Jerusalem, that *My name* may be there." Aerial photographs have confirmed God's Word, for they have captured a phenomenon: God, the great I AM, chiseled His name as He formed the mountains around Jerusalem.

[Jesus] answered and said to [the Pharisees], "I tell you that if these should keep silent, the stones would immediately cry out." (Luke 19:40)

5. The Prophetic Blessing is to be bestowed face-to-face!

Jacob called the name of the place Peniel: "For I have seen God face to face, and my life is preserved." (Genesis 32:30)

So the Lord spoke to Moses face to face, as a man speaks to his friend. (Exodus 33:11)

[The inhabitants of this land] have heard that You, Lord, are among these people; that You, Lord, are seen face to face and Your cloud stands above them, and You go before them in a pillar of cloud by day and in a pillar of fire by night. (Numbers 14:14)

The mandate in Numbers 6:23 states, "Say to them," which means "as a person speaks with his friend face-to-face."³ God spoke with Jacob and Moses face-to-face.

Following His resurrection, Jesus met with His disciples several times face-to-face (Luke 24:36). One who is ready to receive the Prophetic Blessing does so with intent, standing before his or her delegated spiritual authority—face-to-face. When we stand before the Lord in heaven to receive His blessing—"Well done, good and faithful servant"—it will be face-to-face (Matthew 25:23).

6. The Prophetic Blessing is to be given with the voice of authority that all can hear.

The Levites [priests] shall speak with a loud voice and say to all the men of Israel. . . . (Deuteronomy 27:14)

Divine proclamations are not mousy! When you pray, angels are listening and demons are trembling. When you give a prophetic proclamation, all present should be able to hear you. In Judaism, if a rabbi is too weak to speak loudly enough for all to hear, he is not allowed to give the blessing.[4] When you speak anything pertaining to the Word of God, be as bold as a lion, and speak without apology to anyone concerning the core values of your faith.

ARE YOU READY?

Do you want to positively impact the future of your children's lives? Do you want to renew and reenergize your children's marriages? Do you want to breathe hope and prosperity into your children and grandchildren's business and finances? Do you want to break the yoke of illness in your family? Would you like your children to have the unlimited favor of God? You have the power to impact your children's and grandchildren's future for good!

Don't wait a moment longer! Begin to pray for each of your children and grandchildren and ask God to reveal to you what you should pray over their lives. Once you have a clear word from the Lord, then lovingly lay hands on them, proclaim the Priestly Blessing followed by the Prophetic Blessing, and watch God begin to work in their lives!

PART 2

⊰◯⊱

PROCLAMATIONS

Proclamations

Your words have power, for King Solomon declared that "The tongue has the power of life and
death, and those who love it will eat its fruit" (Proverbs
18:21 NIV). Speak the Word of God over your life and
the lives of your children, for King David petitioned
God by saying, "Hear my prayer, O God; give ear to the
words of my mouth" (Psalm 54:2).

There is a miracle in your mouth activated by your
faith in the living Word of God, for Paul proclaims, "By
faith we understand that the worlds were framed by the
word of God, so that the things which are seen were not
made of things which are visible" (Hebrews 11:2–4).
Believe that nothing is impossible for God as you speak
the Prophetic Blessing over your children, for Jesus said,
"The things which are impossible with men are possible
with God." (Luke 18:27).

The following proclamations are inspired by the
Word of God. Declare them over your child, believe
them to be true, and expect them to come to pass—for
you and your children were *born to be blessed!*

Proclaiming the Prophetic Blessing over Your Family

Born to Be Blessed is designed to equip you for declaring God's Word over your life and the lives of your loved ones. Speak the Word of God over your children and grandchildren, over your children's marriages, over their businesses; declare His promises over a child who is sick and needs divine healing, a loved one who is going through a great personal trial, a grandchild in desperate need of emotional stability, a niece or nephew who wants to attack their lack and discover God's prosperity, a child who desires the favor of God.

I offer the following proclamations that will help you begin your exciting journey toward worry-free living. God wants your family to have peace that surpasses understanding, joy that is unspeakable, and love that is boundless, rich, and pure—He wants you to live the good life!

The power and majesty of the Prophetic Blessings of God to His people have been unveiled to you in the first section of this book. God desires to bless your children as you commit your heart and life in full surrender to do His will. When you proclaim God's Word through these Prophetic Blessings, it will supernaturally transform your family for now, for the future, and forever!

THE PRIESTLY BLESSING

Before you proclaim the Prophetic Blessing over your loved ones, begin as the Lord instructed in the book of Numbers (6:24–26) by reciting the Priestly Blessing over them.

> *The LORD bless you and keep you;*
> *The LORD make His face shine upon you,*
> *And be gracious to you;*
> *The LORD lift up His countenance upon you,*
> *And give you peace.*

꜀꜀

PROCLAMATIONS FOR REPENTANCE, FORGIVENESS, AND SALVATION

And they cried out in a loud voice:
"Salvation belongs to our God,
who sits on the throne, and to the Lamb."
REVELATION 7:10 NIV

REPENTANCE

Father, God of Abraham, Isaac and Jacob, You have declared that in repentance lies Your salvation. Thank You Lord for You are ever-faithful and just to forgive us our sins and purify us from all unrighteousness as we repent before You. I proclaim that my child will hear and answer Christ's call to repentance.

May they experience godly sorrow which produces repentance that leads to salvation and leaves no regret. I ask that my child learn to apply the gift of repentance that You have so graciously provided all of Your children. I thank You Lord that Your kindness, mercy, and patience leads my child to repentance, which will produce in them a pure heart, a moral conscience, and a sincere faith. Amen.

FORGIVENESS

The Word declares that with God there is forgiveness and through the shedding of Christ's blood we have redemption, in accordance with the riches of the Father's grace. Lord, there is none like You, for You have promised to forgive our transgressions and remember our sins no more.

Through Your unmerited grace You have extended Your forgiveness to my child for their confessed faults and hidden offenses. May my child have the wisdom, discipline, and strength to forgive others as You have forgiven them for as they forgive, they will be forgiven. May they not judge or condemn and let not their prayers be hindered but let them come before You with a pure heart having forgiven all who have offended them. Amen.

SALVATION

Father God, Your Word declares that all must turn to You in repentance and have faith in the Lord Jesus to be saved. I proclaim that my child will commit their heart, soul, and mind to Jesus Christ for their eternal salvation early in their lives. May God grant them the faith to trust in Him alone for the forgiveness of their sins, the redemption of their soul, and the provision of eternal life through His Son, Jesus Christ, our Savior and Lord. Amen.

RELEASING THE WORD OF GOD INTO YOUR LIFE

In the Name of Jesus, we repent of any ignorance of the Word of God and ask Him to forgive us for the foolish things we have prayed. We bind every hindering force that has been given strength by the words of our mouths, and break the power of those spiritual forces in the mighty Name of Jesus. Through the blood of Jesus, we bind every word that has released the devil or allowed his weapons to come against my child.

I ask that you, my child, receive wisdom and understanding from God to set in motion, through scriptural methods, all that is good, pure, perfect, lovely, and of good report. May you make a covenant with God to pray accurately and speak only that which glorifies Him. Let no corrupt communication proceed from your mouth, but only that which edifies and ministers grace to the hearer.

Do not grieve the Holy Spirit of God, but give glory and honor and praise to the Lord Jesus Christ for all that has been and shall be done for your good and not your harm. The enemy has no power over you! I proclaim that all that is blessed of God and all that God has designed for you shall come to pass in your life.

All the evil, all the bad reports, and all the enemy has designed to deceive you, to lead you astray, and to destroy your home, your finances, or YOU, shall be stopped in the powerful Name of Jesus. My child, you are blessed in the city and blessed in the field. You are blessed in the baskets and blessed in the store. You are blessed in your coming in and your going out. You are the head and not the tail; you are above and not beneath.

You are fully blessed of Almighty God, strengthened with all might according to His glorious power. The Spirit of Truth is in you; He will give you divine discernment, direction, and understanding of every situation and every circumstance of your life. You have the wisdom of God and the mind of Christ, and we thank our heavenly Father for His Spirit, who leads us all. In the precious Name of Jesus we accept all that is promised in God's Holy Word for my child's good.

Proclamations for a Prosperous Spiritual Life

Beloved, I pray that you may prosper in all things
and be in health, just as your soul prospers.

3 John 1:2

WALKING BY FAITH

You are a child of God, declared righteous through faith in Jesus Christ. The life you now live in the body you live by faith in God, who loved you and gave Himself up for you. Walk by faith, my child, not by sight, but trust in the Lord with all your heart and mind and do not rely on your own understanding. In all your ways acknowledge Him, and He will direct your path.

Shut out distractions: focus your love and attention on Jesus, your Redeemer and on the completion of your faith. Saturate yourself in the Word of God and continually listen to the Lord's voice. As you conform to the will of God in thought, word, and deed, your faith will assure you of the things hoped for and is the proof of things you cannot see.

Pray with faith, believing and trusting that when you ask, you will receive; when you seek, you will find; and when you knock, the door will be opened to you. Have faith that He who began a good work in you will continue until the day of Christ's return. May you—by faith—obey God, receive strength, and give praise to the King of kings and Lord of lords!

SUBMISSION

My child, as you submit yourself reverently and completely to God, offer your life as a living sacrifice to

Him. Submit to and trust His discipline as it enables you to share in His holiness. In obedience to God's Word, submit yourself to godly authority for His sake. Honor and respect us, your parents, for this is pleasing to God. Learn His Word and obey it. Remember that as you submit to God and resist Satan, your enemy must flee from you. Trust in the Lord's mercy—and may your heart rejoice in His salvation as you submit to the Lord and to His loving-kindness.

NEARNESS TO GOD

My child, may you be like King David, a person after God's own heart. I bless you, in faith, believing that you will draw ever closer to God, know Him deeply, and long for more of His goodness every day of your life. When you are tired and tempted to lose heart, draw close to the Lord, and He will renew your strength. May the knowledge of His Word bring you discernment, wisdom, and blessings all the days of your life.

MAKING YOUR LIFE A WITNESS FOR CHRIST

May everything you do and say give glory to God, your Father. In all your ways, with kindly affection, give precedence and show honor to others. Have the same attitude, purpose, and humble mind that is in Christ Jesus, for He is our example in humility. Be respectful, self-controlled, and trustworthy in all things. May your tongue declare God's righteousness and His praise all day long—and may the words of your mouth be righteous, pure, and pleasing to Him. As you give thanks to the Lord, may you make known His deeds among the peoples and speak of all His wonders. Seek the Lord and His strength; seek His face continually, and you will be blessed.

HUMILITY

Be clothed with meekness, for God resists the proud but gives grace to the humble. Therefore, humble yourself under the mighty hand of God, that He may exalt you in due time.

HONESTY

I proclaim this Scripture over you, my child: "Whoever desires to love life and see good days, let him keep his tongue from evil and his lips from speaking deceit; let him turn away from evil and do good; let him seek peace and pursue it. For the eyes of the Lord are on the righteous, and his ears are open to their prayer" (1 Peter 3:10–12 ESV).

INTEGRITY

Show yourself in all respects to be a model of decency and uprightness. The righteous person walks in honor; his children are blessed after him. Your godly morals and worthiness will guide you and preserve you as you wait for the Lord.

⊰◯⊱

PROCLAMATIONS FOR WISDOM, PURPOSE, AND GUIDANCE

Let the wise listen and add to their learning,
and let the discerning get guidance.

PROVERBS 1:5 NIV

WISDOM

Wisdom comes from God, and He will give it to you freely when you ask for it. Call on the Lord: He will answer you and show you great and mighty things that you do not know. May your life be blessed as you walk in the skillful wisdom of God, which He has stored away for the righteous. May you continuously seek understanding and knowledge as you walk in reverent fear of the Lord. May God's wisdom bring you His abundant life, which will guard, honor, and promote you.

God's wisdom will produce in you a long life, prosperity, and peace. It is a tree of life—cling to it! And as you cling to God's wisdom, may He give you divine insight regarding the path He has designed for your good.

PURPOSE

You are called by God's Name, created for God's glory, and formed by the One who knew you before you were born. He is acquainted with all your ways and has laid His hand of blessing upon you. May the God who gave you life show you the divine path for which you were created. May you achieve your divine destiny in all the days God has numbered for you.

GUIDANCE

Acknowledge God in all your ways, and He will direct your path. May the Holy Spirit guide you, teach you all things, and bring to remembrance all He has told you. May God's Word be a lamp to your feet and a light to your path. May your soul rest in the assurance and confidence that the Lord's thoughts and ways are higher than your thoughts and ways—and that God's way for you is perfect.

May your steps be directed and established by the Lord because He delights in your way. May the Lord keep His eye on you, counsel you, and instruct you in the way that you should go. May the Lord continually guide you through the rough places, keep you from hidden danger, and make your crooked way straight. He goes before you to show you His path, beside you to accompany you, and behind you to protect you as He presents you blameless to God, the Father.

PROCLAMATIONS FOR FAMILY

Train up a child in the way he should go;
and when he is old he will not depart from it.
PROVERBS 22:6

CHILDBEARING

I speak the Word of God over your womb because the Word of God is alive and full of power; it is active, operative, energizing, and effective. This power of God is fully and completely available to you because you are a believer in the Lord Jesus Christ. Receive and release this immeasurable and unlimited power over your life, knowing with full confidence that God is working in you.

The Lord knows the desire of your heart. I declare in faith that you will become a joyful mother. Just as God gave Isaac to Sarah, He will give you the children you desire. God will release His miraculous provision upon you. You will grow strong and empowered by your faith as you give praise and glory to God who will fully satisfy you, who will keep His Word and do all that He has promised.

NEW LIFE

I proclaim God's blessings over this precious new life He has created in your womb. Children are a heritage from the Lord, and we praise Him for this baby who is being fearfully and wonderfully made. God has created this baby's innermost being and has knit this precious new life together in your womb. God's eyes, even now, see your baby, and He has ordained your baby's life for His glory. May your delivery be safe and quick. May you and your baby be strong and healthy. And may your child be a joy to you every day of your life.

DEDICATING A CHILD TO GOD

Like Hannah, we consecrate your child to God and pray that this new life will be a blessing for your family and the kingdom of God. May your child be blessed of the Lord as they listen to His voice and faithfully keep His commands.

May your child come to know Christ as Savior early in life. I pray that God's power might enable your child to know, through personal experience, the love of Christ and be overtaken with the divine Presence of God Himself.

As an heir to the promise of Abraham, I speak health to your child's body, pray a hedge of protection over your child's mind, and claim God's prosperity upon the work of their hands. May the Lord be with your child wherever they go, leading and holding them by His right hand. May God continually strengthen your child with His mighty power, as the Holy Spirit lives within their innermost being and may your child reflect the love and joy of God all of their days on this earth.

Do not fear, for through the authority of the blood of the Lamb, I bind satan in the mighty Name of Jesus and cancel any assignment against your child. May God guard and keep your child in perfect peace now and forevermore!

YOUR SON

Heavenly Father, God of Abraham, Isaac, and Jacob, as the priest of my house, I place my hands on the head of my son _____ and proclaim this blessing. May he not walk in the counsel of the ungodly, nor stand in the path of the sinful, nor sit in the seat of scorners! May he always delight in Your law and meditate on Your Word day and night. Make him like a tree firmly planted by rivers of water and ready to bring forth its fruit in its season; its leaf also shall not fade or wither, and everything he does shall prosper and come to maturity. I speak and release this blessing over my son _____. Amen.

YOUR DAUGHTER

Heavenly Father, God of Abraham, Isaac, and Jacob, as the priest of my house, I place my hands on the head of my daughter _____ and proclaim this blessing. Let her life be as the life of Ruth—blessed and highly favored in all things. Give to her the desires of her heart, and richly bless everything she puts her hand to.

She is worth more than rubies; her presence brings the light of God into our home. She is clothed with strength and honor, she speaks with wisdom, and the law of love rules the speech of her mouth. Give to my daughter the reward she has earned, and let her excellent works praise her. In Jesus' name, I speak and release this blessing over my precious daughter. Amen!

YOUR GRANDCHILD

Heavenly Father, God of Abraham, Isaac, and Jacob, I place my hands on the head of my grandchild and bless them in Your Holy Name. May they know You early in life as they learn to hear Your voice and obey Your commandments. I ask You, Lord God, to bless my grandchild in their goings out and comings in. May You send Your angels to go before to prepare their way, to protect them from all harm and danger, and to be the rear guard.

Bring to my grandchild godly friends and may the spouse that You have chosen love them second only to You. Bring to my grandchild the blessings of Abraham, Isaac, and Jacob and may everything they do prosper. I ask that You bless my grandchild's heart, soul, mind, and body as they consecrate them to the purposes of God. May Your grace and peace rest upon my grandchild now and forever. In Jesus' name, Amen!

THE SINGLE PARENT
AND THEIR CHILD

Father, You are the Lord of hosts, my child's Maker, and my eternal mate. You nurture, protect, and cherish my child—and will continue to execute justice on my child's behalf.

God, You are the Father of the fatherless, I will not worry about my child's future, for You have promised that the righteous are not forsaken and that their seed will not beg for bread. Grant me wisdom and discernment as I raise my child in the fear and admonition of You. Give me strength for the daily journey I walk and allow me to remember that You will never leave us or forsake us. You have promised to hear us when we cry out, and You have promised to provide for all of our needs and desires!

I declare that we will feel safe, loved, and blessed, for You are our present and eternal Source. Lord, You have promised to uphold and secure our future, giving us hope for tomorrow. May we make You our refuge as You give Your angels charge over us. We will have confidence in You, for you are Jehovah-Jireh, "the Lord our Provider."

TRAINING CHILDREN

Lord, my children are a gift from You. Give me the discipline to daily place them in Your arms as I teach them to walk in Your ways. May Your wisdom guide me as I compassionately train them for the purpose of producing within them the fruit of Your righteousness and holiness.

I declare that I will deal with my children with tenderhearted grace, mercy, kindness, humility, gentleness, and patience. I will stand with my children when they fail, willingly encouraging them, keeping no record of their wrongs, and forgiving them as You have forgiven me. I will teach and impress the Word of God upon their hearts and minds in order to equip them for every good work that You have assigned to them.

PROCLAMATIONS FOR GODLY RELATIONSHIPS

Blessed is the man who walks not in the counsel of the ungodly, nor stands in the path of sinners, nor sits in the seat of the scornful; but his delight is in the law of the LORD, and in His law he meditates day and night.

PSALM 1:1-2

SOCIAL LIFE

I pray that the Lord will bring you only godly friends and associates and will keep you from any influences that would draw you away from Him. Remember that you are a friend of God, and He is your Source of all love and companionship. May all your friendships bring you godly fellowship. May you seek His discernment in your social relationships, for those you associate with will mold your future. May you not be deceived by outward appearances but remember that God looks at the goodness of the heart. May you possess the courage and grace you need to release friendships that keep you from your divine destiny. May you always have a desire to please God instead of pleasing others.

FUTURE SPOUSE

My child, as you wait for your godly spouse, commit your ways to God and rely solely on Him to answer your prayer. Trust in the Lord that He will give you the desire of your heart. Be confident that when you make any request according to God's will, He listens and hears you. We pray for a spouse who will love you second only to Christ. May your future spouse love you as Christ loves the church; nurturing, carefully protecting, and cherishing you forever. The Lord knows the thoughts and plans He has for you, which will give you hope for your future and for your spouse. As you give thanks to God, know that His peace is guarding your heart and mind. May He keep both you and your future spouse pure until you enter into His sacred union.

MARRIAGE

My precious child, as you leave your mother and father to unite with your spouse and become one flesh, know that God has joined you together and that no man can separate you. I pray that you remember these sacred biblical principles: the husband is the head of the home as Christ is the head of the church, the wife is subject to her husband, and the husband will love his wife as Christ loves the church.

May you keep strife out of your marriage, so that there will be no confusion, disharmony, rebellion, or any sort of evil and vile practices within your union. In doing so, your prayers will be effective and not hindered.

Remember that the sacred covenant of marriage is holy to the Lord. May the example of God's love rule your marriage: for it does not envy, it does not parade itself, it is not puffed up, it does not behave rudely, it does not seek its own way, it is not provoked, it thinks no evil, and it does not rejoice in iniquity. Instead, God's love rejoices in truth, is longsuffering, is kind, bears all things, believes all things, and endures all things. This is the kind of love you want in your marriage, for it will never fail you. In Jesus' mighty Name, Amen.

PROCLAMATIONS FOR NEW BEGINNINGS

Though your beginning was small,
yet your latter end would greatly increase.

JOB 8:7

NEW SCHOOL YEAR

As you begin this school year, know that you are God's handiwork, created to do good works and to walk in the paths He has prepared for you. You are ready and equipped for any task through Christ, who fills you with inner strength. He is your sufficiency. The Lord will encourage your heart and strengthen you in every good work and word. God will furnish you with favor and earthly blessings at all times and in all things so that you will accomplish the good works He sets before you.

Whatever you do, whether in word or deed, do it with all your might, in the name of the Lord Jesus, giving praise to God the Father.

NEW JOB

As you begin this new job the Lord has provided for you, obey your employer and those you serve, showing respect and kindness. Work diligently, with all your heart, not to please man, but as if doing service to Christ Himself. Prove yourself to be loyal, faithful, and entirely reliable so that you might do credit to the teachings of God our Savior.

As you commit and trust your work and plans wholly to God, He will cause your thoughts to become agreeable to His will, and He will bless the work of your hands with success. You will work diligently without murmuring, faultfinding, complaining, questioning, or doubting. You will place your trust in God. He will fill you with power and strength when you are weak and tired. Place your hope in Him. You will run and not grow weary. You will walk and not faint. The Lord will make even your enemies have peace with you. May the work of your hands come back to profit you and may you receive honor for your patience, faithfulness, and obedience. You will enjoy the fruit of your labor, for it is a gift from God. For, whatever good you do, you will receive your reward from the Lord.

SUCCESS IN NEW BUSINESS

Heavenly Father, God of Abraham, Isaac, and Jacob, I proclaim today that my child's business is Yours, for every good and perfect gift comes from You. I ask that You would bless my child and enlarge their territory, that Your hand would be with them and that You would keep them from evil that they may not cause others pain or harm.

I confess with my mouth that it is the Lord who gives my child the power to get wealth. It is the Lord who opens the windows of heaven to send blessings to my child that are above and beyond what they can ask or imagine for You delight in the prosperity of the righteous. Whatever my child puts their hand to will prosper for it is the promise of the Lord.

May You close doors that no man can open and

open doors that no man can close. May You bring only righteous people along their path and may You protect them from the Devourer who plans for their destruction. Therefore, Lord God, open the windows of heaven and bless my child's business that Your Name might be glorified and all their needs shall be met.

NEW RELATIONSHIP

As you enter into this new relationship, may you commit it to the Lord, for His glory. Enjoy getting to know each other, but stay free from the temptation of all sexual impurity in thought, word, or deed, accepting that your body is the temple of the Holy Spirit. May this new relationship, from its very beginning, be grounded in God's love and built upon the solid foundation of His Word.

MOVING AWAY FROM HOME

As you follow the Lord's will to move to a new city, I proclaim this Scripture over you, my child: "'I know the plans that I have for you,' declares the LORD, 'plans for welfare and not for calamity to give you a future and a hope'" (Jeremiah 29:11 NASB). As you establish your new home, may God provide a new church family and righteous friends. May He surround you with His protection, blessings, and favor. In Jesus' Name we receive this blessing over your life.

NEW HOME

We praise You, Lord God, for the new home You have provided for my child. "Now therefore, let it please You to bless the house of Your servant, that it may continue before You forever; for You, O Lord GOD, have spoken it, and with Your blessing let the house of Your servant be blessed forever" (2 Samuel 7:29). Fill this new home with Your light, protect those who live here from evil, and may the ones who gather here be surrounded by Your presence and love. May my children continue to proclaim, "As for me and my house, we will serve the LORD" (Joshua 24:15).

⊰◯⊱

Proclamations
of Servanthood

His lord said unto him, Well done, thou good and
faithful servant: thou hast been faithful over a few things,
I will make thee ruler over many things:
enter thou into the joy of thy lord.

Matthew 25:21 kjv

HOSPITALITY

Serve the Lord, my child, with gladness, for you are His handiwork, created in Christ Jesus to do the good works He has planned for you. Serve the Lord with passion, allowing God's light to shine through your worthy deeds so He will be glorified. Arm yourself with the Word of God so you may be equipped for every perfect work.

In both service and spiritual worship, dedicate your body as a living sacrifice, holy, devoted, and well pleasing to God. Work heartily at every task, for you are actually serving the Lord when you minister to others. In kindness and mercy you will do justice to the weak, poor, and fatherless. With love in your heart, you will submit your time, talents, and energy to be used by God in meeting the needs of others, according to His leading.

God will send favor and blessings upon you, my child, and will provide all that you will need to finish every good work in abundance. Cling to God; conform wholly to His example and serve others in His mighty Name.

A CALL TO MINISTRY

As God has called you into ministry, may you be sober in all things, self-controlled, teachable, gentle, and considerate. May you walk in the unmerited favor of God as you minister the Gospel. God has shown you what is good and what He requires of you: to do what is just, to love mercy, and to walk humbly with Him.

May you be in constant prayer, ever mindful that those who are called bear a greater responsibility in the kingdom—maintain righteous judgment according to the degree of faith given by God. Keep your mind and heart in sound doctrine that is nourished by the words of faith. May the Spirit of the Living God continually strengthen you as you show yourself approved.

May the Lord open doors that no man can close and close doors that no man can open as He walks before you to prepare your path, beside you to keep you in all of your ways, and behind you to protect you from the arrows of the evil one.

I proclaim, in faith, that the Holy Spirit will be upon you as you serve with integrity and honesty because He has anointed you to proclaim the Good News and to set at liberty those who are oppressed.

PROCLAMATIONS FOR OVERCOMING ADVERSITY

Be joyful in hope, patient in affliction, faithful in prayer.

ROMANS 12:12 NIV

HOPE FOR A TROUBLED HEART

May you always have hope in God! Don't let your heart be troubled, for remember, my child, that the Lord watches over and protects you during your times of blessing and during your times of affliction. Rejoice in the God of your salvation for He is your strength, your Hope, and your High Tower; He is not far from you; and He will never leave you or forsake you.

The testing of your faith produces patience, which will have its perfect work within you. As you wait upon the Lord He will guide you out of your valley and He will satisfy all of your needs. Praise the Lord when you encounter trouble for you will be complete and lack nothing. Do not fear, be strong, and be encouraged for God will save you; He takes pleasure in those who hope in His mercy.

The Lord is your light and your salvation; whom shall you fear? The Lord is the strength of your life; of whom shall you be afraid? Always set the Lord before you so that your heart will be glad and your flesh will rest in His hope. I proclaim in faith that God will watch over your life and keep you from all harm for He alone makes you to dwell in safety.

Do not be discouraged as you struggle through difficult times but be encouraged for He will win battles on your behalf. It is God's fight not yours. May the

Lord bless you with peace so that you are not anxious about anything even during your time of distress. Be of good courage and hope in the LORD who will renew your strength. You will soar above your circumstances, and you will not become weary or overwhelmed. Offer thanksgiving as you present your requests to God, and His peace will guard your heart and your mind in Christ Jesus.

Be joyful in hope, patient in affliction, and faithful in prayer during your season of adversity. May the Lord fill you with all joy and peace as you trust in Him, so that you may overflow with the power of the Holy Spirit, for the Lord is good and His mercy endures forever! Amen.

LEADING A VICTORIOUS LIFE

Victory is your heritage in Christ. God is with you, and you will have great success in all things. Walk blameless and upright before God, and He will be your Shield and give you the victory over any adversity you face.

Through Christ's life, death, and resurrection you have attained righteousness and strength to achieve great things. I declare that you will remain steadfast, immovable, always abounding in the work of the Lord, knowing that your labor is not in vain. Any evil words or destructive actions formed against you will be powerless and shall fall away.

God will take you from strength to strength and from triumph to triumph, for whatever is born of God is victorious over the world. Give thanks to God who promises to preserve you, deliver you, and give you the victory in all things. Always remember that the greatness, the power, the glory, the victory, and the majesty belong to the Lord. It is His kingdom and He will be exalted as Head over all. The Lord is a God of justice; therefore He shows you His loving-kindness, His grace, and His mercy. You will be blessed, you will be happy, and you will be victorious in Him and through Him.

God has given the power to overcome the enemy because He has promised strength for the day, rest for the weary, grace for the trials, deliverance for the deceived and oppressed, and everlasting and merciful love for your journey. You are more than a conqueror, and you will realize your full potential through Christ who loves you. Declare your triumph, for the favor of God is upon you! Amen.

༺༄༅༎

PROCLAMATIONS FOR HEALING

Praise the LORD, my soul, and forget not all his benefits—
who forgives all your sins and heals all your diseases...

PSALM 103:2–3 NIV

PHYSICAL HEALING

God sent His Word to heal us. Christ was wounded for our transgressions, bruised for our guilt, and by His stripes we are made whole. He promises to hear our prayer, forgive our trespasses, and heal us of our diseases. The Word of God declares that the prayer of faith will save us from sickness and disease. The promises of God hold true: the Promise Keeper of all promise keepers has declared that "many are the afflictions of the righteous but the LORD delivers [us] out of them ALL" (Psalm 34:19)!

The Lord will arise with healing in His wings. He brings forth the restoration and the power of new life. May you, my child, walk in the good news of the Gospel and be healed of every weakness and infirmity as you are made whole by the power of God's Word. Direct us, Lord, to the physicians You have chosen to treat my child; may they possess the mind, the eyes, and the hands of Christ.

Father, God of Abraham, Isaac and Jacob, I know it is Your will, based on Your Word, that the medicine my child takes or the procedures they have will be for their good and not for their harm, for blessed is the Healer of the sick, my Lord and Savior, Jesus Christ.

We thank You, Lord, because what the enemy has hidden in darkness, You have exposed and covered with Your precious blood. Anything that has not been planted by You, Lord, shall be torn up by the roots. Jesus has promised to bind our wounds and heal our afflictions, and He declares that no disease has authority over our bodies.

Father God, You have set before my child life and death. We choose life. You have set before my child blessings and curses. We choose the blessing. Any generational curses that have tormented my family will be revealed and destroyed by the power of Your Word, and You will save my child from the trappings of the evil one and deadly plagues.

May the restoration of my child's body come quickly as Your righteousness goes before them to guide their path and Your glory becomes their rear guard to protect them. Because you have made the Lord your refuge, and the Most High your dwelling place, God will protect you from all evil.

We call upon the Name of the Lord, and He will answer. He will bring to you, my child, supernatural healing, and He will satisfy you with a long and joyful life. Because of the promises found in God's Word, no evil will come against you, for He gives His angels charge over you to accompany, defend, deliver, and preserve you in all your ways.

You were bought with a price. You are free from the curse and have entered into the blessing of Abraham, Isaac, and Jacob—blessings which include good health and favor. The Lord will strengthen, help, and uphold you, my child, with His righteous Right Hand. We give thanks to the Lord for He is good and His mercies endure forever. We declare the greatness of the Lord and bless His name now and forevermore.

EMOTIONAL HEALING

I declare that the Lord will deliver my child out of their distress. He will bind up wounds and heal afflictions. God's understanding is unlimited; He knows the secrets of the heart and mind, and He is full of love and compassion.

May the Lord grant you His peace, my child, at all times and in all ways. Walk in the confidence that the Lord will carry you in His arms and hold you close to His heart. He is always with you and will never leave you or forsake you, and absolutely nothing can separate you from the love of God.

A calm, undisturbed mind and heart are the life and health of your body. You will not be troubled, anxious, or afraid but possess the peace of God that surpasses all understanding. May the Lord God search your heart, try your thoughts, and expose any wickedness, hurt, or offense within you. You will not become angry, disturbed, intimidated, or unsettled, for you are a victorious child of God. You are more than a conqueror through Him who loves you. God did not give you a spirit of fear, but a spirit of power and love, discipline, and self-control.

With the help of the Holy Spirit, you will speak the Word of God over your own life, for God's Word promises protection and peace in times of anxiety; unconditional love and acceptance in times of rejection; understanding and forgiveness in times of anger; faith and hope in times of discouragement; and compassion and joy in times of depression.

Hope is the Helmet of Salvation; you will put it on daily for it will keep you from being double-minded. The mind of Christ Jesus will be yours so that you will conform to His image and gain the discernment and power to reject all futile and idle thoughts. God will keep you in perfect and constant peace because you set your mind on Him. Put your trust in the Lord, for He is a very present help in trouble. As you believe in higher things, think only on the purposes that God has for your life.

May the Lord protect your ears to hear only the voice of the Father and not the lies of the enemy. May your eyes behold only the truth found in God's Word and not the evil of this world. You will choose to think on whatever is noble, just, pure, lovely, and praiseworthy. Remember that no matter how deep the pit, Jesus Christ, your blessed Hope, is deeper still.

SPIRITUAL HEALING

The weapon of warfare designed by God for our victory is not physical but spiritual. This weapon is the infallible Word of the Living God. It is mighty before God, for it defeats and destroys the supernatural bondage that holds you, my child, hostage.

Accept this truth, my child: the Word forgives and redeems you. The Word delivers and transforms you. The Word makes you whole and creates in you a new heart and mind. Christ brought you, my child, out of darkness and shattered the chains that held you. The battle has already been fought and won on your behalf.

You will keep yourself in His holy Word, which will guard your heart, mind, and soul from sin and destruction. As the Word of God declares, we shall pray in the Spirit on all occasions, for it is our prayer that makes God's Word effective in healing us of all our spiritual afflictions, carnal addictions, and emotional torments, for nothing is impossible for Him who loves us.

God delights in the praises of His people. Therefore revere, honor, and worship His majestic holiness. Let His praise be on your lips and in your heart as He intervenes on your behalf. In the precious Name of Jesus we pray and receive these promises. Amen.

꙰

PROCLAMATIONS FOR RECONCILIATION AND RESTORATION

Finally, brothers and sisters, rejoice! Strive for full restoration, encourage one another, be of one mind, live in peace. And the God of love and peace will be with you.

2 CORINTHIANS 13:11 NIV

RECONCILIATION

Through the Blood of Christ my child is reunited with God and reconciled with man so that their prayers may not be hindered. Through the shed blood of Christ my child was made one with God, who is the Author of reconciliation. As Christ's ambassador, my child will represent the love of Christ, in word and deed, bringing unity and peace to family and friends. Thank You Lord for You have reconciled my child to God the Father by Your shed blood.

RESTORATION

God restores through the power of His holy Word, therefore be transformed by the renewing of your mind so that you may accomplish His perfect will for your life. He will give you a new heart and plant in you a new spirit which will shine forth as Christ's transforming light.

Christ restores through the power of His shed blood, which redeems, delivers, and makes righteous. He promises to give back the years that the enemy has taken from you without condemnation or reproach. May you be delivered daily from sin's dominion through Christ's resurrected life. You have been crucified with Christ, and it is no longer you who lives, but Christ who lives within you.

He will complete the good work He began in your life. Know, understand, and realize that God is with you and that He is the Lord, He will restore your life, and there is none like Him.

🙰

PROCLAMATIONS FOR PROTECTION AND SAFETY

But let all who take refuge in you be glad; let them ever sing for joy. Spread your protection over them, that those who love your name may rejoice in you.

PSALM 5:11 NIV

APPLYING THE BLOOD OF CHRIST

I apply the blood of Jesus Christ on the doorpost of my household. Generational curses must pass over my life and the lives of my loved ones because of the power of the Blood of Jesus Christ! No weapon that has been formed against me will prevail because of the supernatural protection of the Blood of the Lamb!

Father, forgive me for underestimating the power of the Blood of Your Son! I acknowledge this day that there is NOTHING that the Blood of Christ cannot do!

The Blood saves; it rescues. The Blood redeems; it has paid the price for my sin. The Blood delivers; it liberates and frees from all forms of curses. The Blood protects; it is a shield that guards, defends, and cares for me and my family. The Blood provides; it grants and supplies all of my needs. The Blood heals; it makes me and mine well. The Blood restores; it reinstates, refurbishes, repairs, and renovates. The Blood transforms; it converts and makes over. The Blood provides everlasting life that is eternal, ceaseless, and perpetual.

As for me and my house: the line has been drawn and the Blood of the Sacred Lamb has been applied! Satan is fully aware of the power of the Blood of Christ; therefore he has no choice but to pass over the household that has placed the Blood of the Lamb on its doorpost. He may try to rob, kill, and destroy as he passes, but it will be for naught because I have declared that Christ is our Redeemer and Deliverer and by His priceless Blood I am protected!

DIVINE PROTECTION

The Lord is your protection, and as a child of God, you live in His presence; therefore the Lord will go before you and behind you to hem you in, and His hand will always be upon you. You will find refuge under His wings, and when you call on the name of Jesus—He will draw near to you, hear your cries, and save you.

In times of danger, He is your shield. The Lord's name is a strong tower—safe and high above all evil. Bring your petitions to the Lord, with thanksgiving, and His peace will surround your heart and mind. When battles come your way, do not be afraid or dismayed because the battles belong to God and He is with you.

When the enemy comes against you like a flood, the Spirit of the Lord will lift up His standard and put him to flight. The Lord is faithful! He is your refuge and fortress! You will lean on Him, rely on Him, and trust in Him. May you find strength in God, for He is your firm Foundation who promises to protect you from all evil and harm. I declare these promises in the Name of our Savior and Lord, Jesus Christ.

SAFE TRAVELING

Father, God of Abraham, Isaac, and Jacob, I ask that You guide, direct, and support my child with Your peace and protection while on their journey. I ask that You allow them to reach their destination with joy and safety, and return them home with the same measure.

May You travel before them to direct their path, walk beside them so they may not journey alone, and stand behind them to keep them safe from any harm. I ask that You give Your angels charge over my child to guard them in all their ways.

My child, I declare blessings on your journey; may the Lord preserve your going out and your coming in from this time forth, and forevermore. May you always walk in God's kindness and favor, for He is good and His mercies endure forever.

꧁꧂

PROCLAMATIONS FOR DIVINE PROSPERITY AND FAVOR

May the favor of the Lord our God rest on us;
establish the work of our hands for us—
yes, establish the work of our hands.

PSALM 90:17 NIV

DIVINE PROSPERITY

Heavenly Father, God of Abraham, Isaac, and Jacob, I come to You as Your servant who believes in, trusts in, and relies on You as my hope and my confidence. Your Word promises to grant Your children an abundance of divine prosperity. The Lord will give me and mine the desires of our hearts as we delight in Him.

My God shall supply all our needs according to His riches in glory by Christ Jesus. Prosperity will come to my household as we submit to God and are at peace with Him. As we obey and serve the Lord, we will spend the rest of our lives in prosperity and contentment. He will not withhold any good thing from us who walk before Him in integrity and honesty.

My child will seek You with all their heart and they will prosper in their mind, soul, and body. As my child pursues God's wisdom and righteousness, they will receive riches, honor, enduring wealth, and prosperity. My child will obey all that the Lord commands so they may live in the Lord's goodness all the days of their lives. Your Word declares that wealth, honor, strength, and authority will be theirs in all things as they heed Your voice and obey Your commandments.

You have provided wealth for my child and they will honor You, Father God, with a tenth of their first fruits. As You have blessed them, they will sow generously into the kingdom of God and will be a blessing to others. Father God, You promise to provide and multiply my child's resources and increase the fruits of Your righteousness in their lives, including goodness, kindness, and charity.

Those who fear and take refuge in You will receive an abundance of good things that you have stored up for them. We will praise You, for You give my child the ability to produce wealth as You, open the floodgates of heaven and pour out abundant blessings upon them that they will not be able to contain.

FAVOR OF GOD

Heavenly Father, God of Abraham, Isaac, and Jacob, I come before You today as Your child seeking Your divine favor for my family. Your Word affirms that You will keep Your Holy covenant with us, and we declare that we will heed Your voice and obey Your mandates. Lord, You promise to look upon us and remember us with Your unmerited favor and make us fruitful in all things.

In the name of Jesus, I proclaim that my child is the righteousness of God; therefore, they are entitled to covenant kindness and favor. The favor of God is among the righteous, and His favor surrounds the righteous; therefore, it surrounds them as a shield.

As my child finds favor in the eyes of God, I expect divine blessings to be manifested everywhere my child goes and in everything they do. Never again will my child be without the favor of God. Satan, my child's days of lack and want cease today! My child will go from the pit to the palace because the favor of God rests richly on them. The favor of God profusely abounds in them.

My child is part of the generation that will experience the immeasurable, limitless, and surpassing favor of God. God's favor will produce in their life supernatural increase, promotion, prominence, preferential treatment, restoration, honor, increased assets, and recognition. Petitions will be granted for their benefit, policies and rules will be changed for my child's good, and You, Father God, will win battles on their behalf that they will not have to fight.

As for me and my house, we will serve and obey the Lord and He will grant us His favor and give us a good name in the sight of man. We will remain humble and contrite in spirit and show reverence for His Word. The favor of God is upon my family and me; it goes before us and lasts a lifetime, and therefore we will never be the same again!

A Parting Blessing

We have completed a life-changing journey that has taken us through the scriptural history of the Prophetic Blessing. We have discovered the importance of releasing and receiving the blessing in both word and deed. We have learned how to declare the spoken word over our lives and the lives of our children. What next?

We must accept the promises of God for our lives found in His holy Word. We need to believe that we were born to bless and *be blessed!* We must learn to hear His voice and live by His mandates so that our lives and the lives of our family members will experience the overwhelming favor of God.

I leave you with a blessing that encompasses many of God's promises for you and your loved ones. Declare it with your voice and believe it in your heart, for His Word is true, powerful, personal, and everlasting. Remember this truth: you were *born to be blessed*!

May the God of Abraham, Isaac, and Jacob bless us with supernatural strength, divine health, and everlasting joy. May He surround us with His safety and protection, in our goings in and our comings out. May our lives be free from any form of curse so that we can receive every blessing that God ordained for us. May we abide in the majesty of His grace and mercy and may His favor continually go before us and our loved ones. May the peace of the Lord fill our lives and guard our hearts. May the Father's enduring love keep us and our beloved families in all of our ways. And may God always smile upon us and may His presence be our daily reward. Amen.

Notes

CHAPTER 1: WHAT IS THE PROPHETIC BLESSING?

1. Tim Hegg, "The Priestly Blessing," Nisan 4, 5761, *Bikurie Zion* 2001; http://www.torahresource.com/EnglishArticles/Aaronic%20Ben.pdf. All rights reserved.
2. Reverend William Bythel Hagee, Dedication Prayer over Pastor John Hagee, October 4, 1987.

CHAPTER 2: THE PROPHETIC BLESSING IN SCRIPTURE

1. "Abortion Statistics," *National Right to Life* (1973-2010); http://www.nrlc.org/Factsheets/FS03_AbortionInTheUS.pdf.

CHAPTER 3: RELEASING THE BLESSING THROUGH THE SPOKEN WORD

1. Robyn Freedman Spizman, *Chief Joseph: When Words Matter Most* (New York: Crown Publishers, 1996), 67.
2. E. C. McKenzie, *Mac's Giant Book of Quips and Quotes* (Eugene, OR: Harvest House Publishers, 1980), 562.
3. Ibid.
4. John Phillips, *Exploring Genesis: An Expository Commentary* (Grand Rapids, MI: Kregel Publishers, 2001), 40.
5. Ibid.
6. Wilbur M. Smith, *Therefore Stand* (Grand Rapids, MI: Baker Book House, 1976), as cited by John Phillips in *Exploring Genesis*, 42.
7. Derek Prince, *The Power of Proclamation* (Charlotte, NC: Derek Prince Ministries-International, 2002), 11.
8. Ibid., 14.
9. Ibid., 11.
10. George Robinson, *Essential Judaism* (New York: Pocket Books, 2000), 26.

CHAPTER 4: RELEASING THE BLESSING THROUGH PHYSICAL TOUCH

1. Tiffany Field, *Touch* (Cambridge, MA: MIT Press, 2003), 17.
2. Mic Hunter and Jim Struve, *The Ethical Use of Touch in Psychotherapy* (Thousand Oaks, CA: Sage Publications, 1998), 13.
3. Ibid.
4. Ibid., 14.
5. Ibid.
6. Ibid.
7. Ibid.
8. Gary Smalley and John Trent, *The Gift of the Blessing* (Nashville, TN: Thomas Nelson, 1993), 45.
9. Ibid.
10. John D. Garr, *Blessings for Family and Friends* (Atlanta, GA: Golden Key Press, 2009), 30.
11. Field, *Touch*, 29.
12. Ibid., 30.
13. Garr, *Blessings for Family and Friends*, 14.
14. Thayer and Smith, *The New Testament Greek Lexicon*, "Ektrepho," public domain.
15. Field, *Touch*, 62.
16. Ibid., 63.
17. Ibid.
18. Ibid.
19. Ibid., 60.

CHAPTER 5: HOW TO RELEASE THE PROPHETIC BLESSING OVER YOUR CHILDREN

1. Adapted from a personal story written by John and Diana Hagee, *What Every Man Wants in a Woman; What Every Woman Wants in a Man* (Lake Mary, FL: Charisma House, 2005), 50-51.
2. Tim Hegg, "The Priestly Blessing," Nisan 4, 5761, *Bikurie Zion* 2001; http://www.torahresource.com/EnglishArticles/Aaronic%20Ben.pdf. All rights reserved.
3. Ibid.
4. Ibid.

ABOUT THE AUTHOR

John Hagee is the author of four *New York Times* bestsellers, in addition to *Jerusalem Countdown*, which sold over one million copies. He is the founder and senior pastor of Cornerstone Church in San Antonio, Texas, a nondenominational evangelical church with more than twenty thousand active members, as well as the founder and president of John Hagee Ministries, which telecasts his radio and television teachings throughout America and in 249 nations worldwide. Hagee is also the founder and national chairman of Christians United for Israel, a national grassroots association with over one million members to date.

WORTHY

PUBLISHING

If you enjoyed this book, will you consider sharing the message with others?

- Mention the book in a Facebook post, Twitter update, Pinterest pin, or blog post.

- Recommend this book to those in your small group, book club, workplace, and classes.

- Head over to www.facebook.com/JohnHageeMinistries, "LIKE" the page, and post a comment as to what you enjoyed the most.

- Tweet "I recommend reading #BorntobeBlessed by @ PastorJohnHagee // @worthypub"

- Pick up a copy for someone you know who would be challenged and encouraged by this message.

- Write a review on amazon.com, bn.com, goodreads.com, or cbd.com.

You can subscribe to Worthy Publishing's newsletter at www.worthypublishing.com

WORTHY PUBLISHING
FACEBOOK PAGE

WORTHY PUBLISHING
WEBSITE